the WOMAN'S BOOK *of* CREATIVITY

the WOMAN'S BOOK of CREATIVITY

C DIANE EALY, Ph.D.

A Beyond Words book in association with

CELESTIALARTS

Berkeley, California

A Beyond Words book in association with
Celestial Arts
P.O. Box 7123
Berkeley, California 94707

Distributed in Canada by Ten Speed Canada, in the United Kingdom and Europe by Airlift Books, in New Zealand by Southern Publishers Group, in Australia by Simon & Schuster Australia, in South Africa by Real Books, and in Singapore, Malaysia, Hong Kong, and Thailand by Berkeley Books.

Typesetting by Pacific Rim Publishing & Design
Design by Principia Graphica

Library of Congress Cataloging-in-Publication Data
on file with the publisher

First Celestial Arts printing, 1999
Printed in Canada

1 2 3 4 5 6 7—03 02 01 00 99

to my mother
Margaret Helen Steele Ealy
who has a genius for raising creative people

to my father
Robert Glenn Ealy
who taught me that there are no mistakes

to **Gray**
for being in my life

Contents

Acknowledgments   ix

Introduction   xi

Notes from the Author   xiii

Part One: Understanding Feminine Creativity

In the Beginning . . .   3

Getting Down to the Roots: What Is Creativity?   11

The Holistic Process: Its Praises and Pitfalls   19

The Outline Doesn't Have to Happen First   27

Finishing What You Start   31

Learning to Change Reality   35

Understanding Your Feminine Nature   39

Part Two: Developing Your Unique Process

Keep It Private—For a While   49

Be Prepared for Provoking a Response   57

Learning to Accept Nurturance   65

Quieting the Inner You   73

Developing a Sense of Timing   79

A Room of Your Own   83

Perfectionism: Creativity's Saboteur   89

Understanding the Creative/Depressive Cycle   97

Where's the Passion?   105

Anger: Creativity's Wrecking Ball   111

Altering Your Sense of Time   119
Expanding Your Sense Of Self   125

Part Three: Integrating Creativity into Your Daily Life

Becoming a Creative Problem-Solver   135
Honoring the Unmeasurable   143
Redefining Power   147
Exercising Your Imagery   153
Ha-Ha = Aha!   161
Becoming More Spontaneous   165
Making the Ordinary Extraordinary   169
Preventing Burnout   173
Loving Your Creative Self   181
Letting Your Dreams Create for You   187
Nurturing Your Talent   197
Is It Quicksand or a Rock?   203

Part Four: Breaking Blocks

Overcoming Blocks   211
Getting Started   215
Procrastination and Creativity—Working Together   221
Quieting the Inner Critic   229
Dealing with Society's Shoulds   235
Dancing with Goliath   241

Concluding Thoughts   247

Notes   251
Bibliography   255
Further Readings   259

Acknowledgments

During the long years of working to get this book published, I am fortunate to have had the support of my family and many friends. And throughout the publishing process, I am blessed to have been working with Cindy Black, Kate McKern, Lisa Schneiderman, Steve Gardner, Richard Cohn, and the rest of the staff at Beyond Words, a truly remarkable company. Special thanks to Julie Livingston for her belief in this book.

Liz MacDonell is an extraordinary editor who always knew how to make my writing better. I owe profound gratitude to Jean Houston, my ever-patient mentor without whom this book would not exist. My life is better for having known her. Judith Allen was always ready to give her feedback on my writing and to keep me from going astray when the agony of this process overtook the joy.

Lynn Taber-Borcherdt, Byrd Baylor, and Barbara Mettler are three exceptionally creative women whose openness and support helped launch this project in the right direction.

I thank Elizabeth Knappman for her belief in this book, Nancy Solomon for her vision, Bernadette Steele for helping me see my strengths, Jacqueline Sharkey for saying the right thing at the right time, Alison Hughes for her insight, and Sereta Robinson and Kay Lesh for their steadfast friendship.

I especially want to thank Mary Ann Brehm, Linda Ehmann, Julie Goebel, Andrea Gold, Lillian Hodkins, Ginia Long, Marjory Vals Maud, Portia Nelson, Ellen Nordberg, Ursula Williams, and the rest of the women who requested anonymity and who participated in this book through their responses to my questionnaire. Your openness and honesty were invaluable.

I am grateful that my family—Gary, Betty, Damon, and David Ealy—have always encouraged me to be who I am and have always laughed at my jokes.

I am a better person because all these dear people are in my life.

Introduction

I have long been fascinated by how we humans participate in our own evolution. Our growth process always seems to be happening in two directions at the same time: back to who we were originally—our true selves; and forward to what we can become—fulfilling that true self. My curiosity led me into the field of creativity. I found that as we embrace our personal development, we embrace our creative selves. This is inevitable.

I have been listening to women talk about their creative process for years. And I am always amazed by how many of them describe wonderfully rich experiences with their creativity and then tell me they don't see themselves as being creative! These women dismiss, discount, and rob themselves of their most powerful aspect, the characteristic which defines who they uniquely are as individuals—their creativity. So if it does nothing else I want this book to help you validate your creative process. That's important to me.

Some women tell me they get in the way of their creative development by spreading themselves too thin, by allowing too much structure into their lives, or by being caught up in, as one businesswoman put it, "busy-ness." Other women permit negativity to interfere with their creativity. They listen to the voices of people who tell them they can't or shouldn't or won't. At the same time, they tell me they overcome these distractions by making time for daily prayer and meditation. They give themselves the time and space to reconnect with who they truly are, at a core level.

Sometimes when I speak with groups of women about their creativity, describing and acknowledging this distinctive process, I see women weep. It's the first time they've heard anyone telling them that how they think and create are OK, even if these processes are different from what we've been told they should be. Those tears are powerful.

Once in a while men have attended my presentations, and several men have read this book. I get positive feedback from them. They tell me that they, too, can relate to much of what I'm saying. I hope you will share this with the men in your life and I hope it brings greater understanding and an opening of communication between you. I'm addressing women's creativity here because I have studied women's process. Understanding the totality of men's creativity is also important.

What's vital about our creative process is that we learn to use it, to nurture it and express it in our daily lives. I'm convinced that an important part of women's nature is that we live creatively. This means our lives are an expression of who we are, of how we choose to define ourselves. I hope this book will help you on your journey into the creative lifestyle.

C Diane Ealy, Ph.D.

$\mathcal{N}$otes from the Author

$\mathcal{A}$s you read this book, you will find words and images in the margins which are designed to facilitate the flow and organization of ideas presented here. The words indicate themes, such as *trust*, *power*, *nurturing yourself*, *careers*, and *challenges*, running throughout the book. Key concepts are marked with a ☞. Longer quotations from creative women are noted with " ". Activities that can assist the reader in enhancing creativity are indicated with a 〰.

Because of the holistic nature of this book, the reader is often referred to previous or upcoming sections which relate to the section being read. To facilitate locating the reference, a ◀ is used to indicate a previous section and a ▶ is used to indicate an upcoming section. In the margin these references are marked with a ◉ or a ◉.

About Mavee

I watch my cat
outdoors
sharpening the claws of her instinct
on Nature
she grows from the earth
alert
ears perked—she won't miss a sound
eyes keen—she won't miss a movement

she munches grass
"Eating grass helps cats . . ." do something
she rises, a floating gray mist
freezing ready
patient, she watches
eons of survival surge through her
precise timing wedded to precise movements

she springs
or did the earth push her
the lizard struggles a little
I wince and forcefully mumble "nature"
presumably the cat is victorious
I do not watch anymore
but return to my room
to write about women's nature

Part One
Understanding
Feminine Creativity

$\mathcal{I}$n the Beginning . . .

A Child's Myth

I learned early who the heroes were: men who went into the world, bravely overcoming evil and whipping the bad guys. They had fun, great adventures. Occasionally they had some help, but ultimately, in those last moments of high drama—the life-or-death, good-shall-prevail struggle—the hero fought alone.

And I was the Hero. In my imagination I was the Lone Ranger, riding through blistering deserts and across endless plains, silver bullets flying, certain of my destiny—to right wrongs. Never mind that my horse was a chair or that my silver bullets were plastic. Or that snow fell outside.

On my way home from school I was Superman. Arms outstretched, cape flying behind me, swooping and soaring through the back streets of my small hometown. Impervious to harm, I extended magnanimous assistance to all in need. Sometimes the top button of my pale yellow sweater came loose and my "cape" fell off. I would brush away clinging dirt and leaves, button it around my neck, and resume my hero status. Easy for a nine-year-old.

Like many other young women, I continued to imitate the male Hero. I conquered things outside myself, alone and proud of my externalized power. I was tough and decisive. But in my late twenties I began to hear an increasingly loud inner voice telling me something was wrong. I started looking at popular heroes' journeys.

By now these fictional heroes were venturing into space, not just barren deserts, but the scenario was the same. The hero—still a he—was fated to journey into uncharted, mysterious worlds, charged with saving the human race, freedom, the planet Earth, or some other equally cherished item. He was armed with an array of weapons and a few faithful friends. And, of course, he was always successful, returning to cheers and grateful praise.

The scenario bothered me. For all his adventures, in spite of coming face-to-face with his own mortality, he returned apparently unchanged. He had more pride, perhaps, more confidence for having conquered some unknown, but essentially he seemed to remain the same. The hero who had been my role model as a child showed himself to be without depth of feeling, void of innate wisdom. I came to realize that if I continued to pursue the male role model I had adopted, I would also stay on that conquering surface. I, too, might be confident but unfeeling.

Many women have believed that same story: If we adopt men's thinking style, imitate men's creativity, behave in the world as men do, then we will succeed as men have. Many women have built careers guided by this belief. Yet I see increasing numbers of successful women challenging this definition of success—asking questions about their identity, independent of accepted roles. They have learned that their success can be unfulfilling and incomplete.

We know now that the Male as Hero story is a false model for women. Imitating this model can be unhealthy and can keep women from becoming who they truly are. One highly successful woman who defines herself in the male model said to me recently, "I enjoy my career, but I'm not as lovable as I used to be. And I don't like that." She has discovered that adopting a style that is unnatural to her gives her many external accomplishments but no inner satisfaction.

A Woman's Reality

There is another perspective, another hero's journey. In this scenario, the hero is a she. Unlike her male counterpart, she has no intentions of conquering anything external. Instead, her journey is within. She travels into the spiraling depths of her own unknowns, constantly discovering and changing in the process. Her intention is to become self-defined.

The female hero reaches full individual potential, taking enormous personal risks, orchestrating many times the death of her former self and nurturing the emergence of a new, more integrated self. The female hero is the woman living a creative lifestyle. Her discovery is the unfolding of the self-defined, creative woman who lives within each of us.

A remarkable gift, creativity. No other natural aspect of the human psyche is as powerful. It can exist unused for many years and then, with the right encouragement, creativity can be expressed, improving our lives and the lives of everyone around us.

A woman's creative process is unique. We must understand our creative nature to know how to nurture it and use it wisely. We also need tools for coping with problems that can result from our distinctive creative process.

The Linear Approach

I began my exploration into creativity accepting what all of the creativity researchers believed—that studying creativity makes a person more creative! I thought the field itself would be creative. But I quickly learned that virtually all creativity research is based on a four-step linear model that was developed by studying the thinking processes of noted scientists, mathematicians, and the like. Psychologist Graham Wallas first published this paradigm in *The Art of Thought* in 1926.[1] And creativity researchers, desperate for a model, grabbed onto it and apparently hadn't questioned it since. But it bothered me.

The four steps consist of preparation, incubation, illumination, and verification. In the *preparation* stage, all important information is gathered. Next, in the *incubation* stage, this information is put on the mind's "back burner" so the unconscious can work on the issue. The *illumination* phase is marked by the *aha!* of having the solution suddenly present itself. The final stage, *verification*, simply means giving an outward form to the creative idea.

Wallas's creativity model was based only on men; women were entirely excluded from his study. And while I recognized these stages in my own experience with certain levels of my thinking process, I couldn't relate to them as being representative of my creative process. That happens at a much different level than the linear model represented. I wondered if other women might share my experience.

The studies about brain function that I had found as a graduate student showed a possibility for women's and men's brains developing differently.[2, 3, 4] The bottom-line effect, the research suggested, is that women have a preference for a more holistic thinking style while men tend toward the linear. In addition, stories from Greek and Roman mythology also portray women as favoring more all-inclusive approaches while men seem more comfortable with step-by-step approaches. ▶ Again I was curious: If women think holistically, do we create holistically as well?

I also knew that if a holistic process were to be viewed through a linear lens, that process would probably not be understood, recognized, or appreciated. Creativity is a personal and complicated process, and I was suspicious of reducing it down to only four steps.

See
Understanding Your Feminine Nature
p. 39

When I put these pieces together—the linear model, heavy reliance on men for that model, women's apparent preference for holistic thinking—I was not surprised when I found statements by leading researchers indicating their belief that women aren't creative.

One of the most often quoted researchers is Frank Barron, who, in 1968, called it "historical fact" that "intellectual creativity has been conspicuously lacking in women, whose products are their children."[5] He further wrote that women having children and men having ideas, paintings, and other creative forms was Nature's division of labor. He also suggested that women who engage in the kind of creative work usually done by men may have "some degree of reversal of the usual sexual identifications." The source for these quotes, a book ironically entitled *Creativity and Personal Freedom*, has been frequently quoted for the last thirty years.

Another often-cited work is *Development of the Creative Individual*, by John Gowan, who acknowledged that his book was based on the development of creativity in males. He noted, "The reason for leaving out female development is ignorance on our part, not prejudice."[6] However, he referred to a study showing that children between the ages of four and seven who identify with their opposite-sexed parent are more likely to be creative as adults. He said, "Because more boys are close to their mothers during this period (closer than girls are to their fathers) may be one explanation why there later are more creative men than women in the world of adults."[7]

But he offered no proof to support his conclusion. Was he operating on the commonly held assumption that a tangible product has to result from creative effort? Conflict resolution, personal growth, motivating others, and other intangible products arise from the creative process of many women. If these products aren't recognized as creative, neither are the people who create them.

The New Perspective

If the above examples were dead and gone, we might chalk them up to being relics of a bygone era; however, these quotes are twenty-five years old but the beliefs still linger. Creativity research hasn't gotten particularly creative in recent years. The four-step approach is still revered. Ignorance of a different creative process remains the norm.

The woman's creative process has never been fully explored, honored for its special characteristics, or understood. When I conducted my first studies into women's creativity, I knew I was studying a different culture, so I resisted making any assumptions about the creative process as women experience it. I wanted to understand it from their perspective.

Because I have studied women, I talk exclusively about women's creativity. Does this mean that I'm saying men don't create in ways similar to women? No, it doesn't. What it does mean is that there is more than one way of being creative. In the past, studies relying primarily on men and men's processes have been generalized to the entire population. As a result, women are held to a male standard of behavior. I see no reason to perpetuate the error—or create a *new* misconception—by saying that because women create differently from the commonly accepted linear model, then men must create this way too.

I even have my doubts that the traditional four steps accurately represent the deep creative process in men; they certainly fail to describe women's experience.

Status quo has resulted in women often having negative views of our creativity. We discount our distinctive processes and our self-esteem suffers. Our contributions to society are thereby minimized, discouraging us from developing our creativity and inhibiting us from seeking appropriate financial rewards when we are creative.

But we can change this situation. One of the most remarkable aspects of this age is that a single individual's actions make a difference to the whole. As you nurture creativity in one area of your life, it begins to flourish in other areas.

The expression of women's creativity is crucial to our development as self-defined individuals who understand that real power is having power over ourselves. This knowledge negates the old notion of power as something held over someone else. Creative women are strong women who empower others through their creativity.

If you want to be more creative, you exercise creativity, just as you strengthen your body by exercising. You can channel your creative energy in any direction—into your workplace or home. You may want to express your artistic talents more fully or to live a creative lifestyle, continually taking in new experiences and information and making them part of your life.

This book weaves content and process as they are woven in our lives. In my life, I use a spiral logic where ideas and feelings are connected, resolved, and used as building blocks. Then I find myself—as perhaps you do too from time to time—re-examining those thoughts and feelings from a different perspective. I find myself at a new level of the spiral where I have more information, new feelings about old thoughts, and new insights. Or I've reconfirmed my previous ideas.

Have you ever believed you resolved an issue, only to have it recur? This is the spiral at work. It gives us the opportunity to examine the old from a new perspective, from a new point on the spiral. This phenomenon happens no matter where we start on the spiral and no matter which direction we're going at the moment. Have deep respect for your spiraling process. As we travel inward on our creative journey, we ultimately know ourselves better.

Use this book as it's convenient for you. Read it from front to back, using the activities in each section. Or skip from one topic to another as you feel you need to develop the skills discussed in that chapter. With a holistic, spiraling process, you can start in the middle or the end or anywhere you choose. Remember, creativity doesn't necessarily start with *A* and then go to *B* and then to *C*. Neither does this book.

As you explore and develop your creativity, there may be times when you feel isolated. Creative people often are alone in their vision and ideas. When you feel alone on your path, remember that the journey is shared. I present nothing here that I haven't been through myself, with women in workshops and seminars, and in private sessions.

This book is intended to be savored over time rather than to be consumed in one sitting. Allow yourself time to experience the information and the activities. Some of these exercises may stir up unexpected issues for you. If this happens, I urge you to seek the guidance of a trusted therapist who can facilitate your continued growth.

Regardless of your approach, I intend to challenge you to find ways you are creative. I want you to catch yourself acting creatively every day and to acknowledge and celebrate those acts. I want you to feel energized by your creative spirit the moment you awaken each morning and to be nurtured by that energy throughout the day. Your creativity is yours to use and to direct. This book will help you do both.

Getting Down to the Roots: What Is Creativity?

What Is Your Definition?

Many definitions of the creative process exist. Some revolve around a tangible product, like a book or painting or sculpture. Others involve the notion that any new thought, as long as it's new to the creator, is a result of the creative process. And other definitions focus on the process itself, describing what an individual experiences during the creative act. But your personal definition is the most important, because it lies at the root of whether you think of yourself as a creative individual—and to what degree. Try this brief activity:

> Take a piece of paper (or use the inside flap of this book) and complete this sentence:
> "For me, creativity is . . . ."

Don't allow yourself to say, "I'm not creative." Women often follow that statement with, "I don't paint pictures or write books," as if the creative process must result in an item. This attitude stifles creativity. If your definition of creativity says that all creative products are concrete, then here's your first opportunity to expand your thinking!

The results of women's creative efforts are often intangible, but they are still substantial. Have you ever helped people resolve a conflict, enabled a group to learn, incorporated new learning into your behavior, or solved a perplexing problem? You've been creative. And the result is equal to any book or painting or sculpture. It's the newness and joining of previously unrelated ideas or feelings that count.

Take a look at your definition again. If it doesn't allow for intangible products, change it. Think about times when you devised a new way to deal with a troublesome individual or motivated someone to action. Can you see yourself now in your expanded definition? Good. The first step in exercising your creativity is envisioning yourself as creative. Creativity exists in every healthy human being. Acknowledge yours.

Common Misconceptions

In 1980 *The Wall Street Journal* conducted a nationwide survey of 782 chief executives from all sizes of companies to determine what qualities they would look for in their replacements.[1] Integrity was first on the list. Other frequently listed traits were: ability to get along with others, ability to plan, capacity to recognize and solve problems, independence, and ability to see the whole picture. All of these qualities describe a creative person, yet creativity doesn't appear on the list! Why? Because labeling a person as "creative" can erroneously cast a negative light on that individual as someone who would be a constant source of disturbance within an organization.

Interestingly, throughout the '80s and '90s numerous books written for the business world have focused on the need for creativity at all levels. Companies are being urged to nurture innovation among employees while managers are encouraged to develop their intuition. Still, in some industries words like *innovative* are more frequently used than *creative*, as if suspicions still surround this distinctive ability.

Many books have also been written on the connection between mental instability and creativity, leading to the common misconception that one is a function of the other. This connection is unfortunate and completely misleading. I want to dispel this idea.

True, some highly creative people have also been psychotic. But it doesn't follow that creativity springs from psychosis or vice versa. Too often we assign creativity to the extremes of madness—such as Van Gogh—or of genius—as with Einstein. These concepts serve to separate us from our creativity because no one can identify with the mental instability of a suicidal artist or the extreme intellect of an inventor and look forward to a lifetime of healthy creative expression. Being creative is communicating a completely healthy, natural part of ourselves. Tie your definition to your most positive aspects.

Know that sometimes people are suspicious of creative individuals. Be glad! While creative people do challenge the status quo, we are also agents for change, for the improvement of life in general.

Check your feelings about these ideas. If you have any negative concepts about being creative, they will inhibit your development.

An excellent way to rid yourself of negative thoughts and feelings is to externalize them, to bring them out of you. Try the sentence-completion activity again, only this time instead of writing a definition, unload any negative thoughts you might have about creativity. Complete these sentences:

"Creativity . . . ." or "Creative people . . . ."

You may want to vary the words to suit your needs. For example: "If I'm creative at work, people will think I'm weird" or "Work and creativity don't mix" or "Creative people are troublemakers."

I recommend writing your thoughts on separate sheets of paper. When you are finished, destroy these distracting ideas in three steps: write CANCEL across the statements, tear the sheets into pieces, then destroy them. You might try burning the papers and flushing the ashes down the toilet or burying them under a beautiful plant. However you choose to do it, the point is to free yourself from the negative thoughts. With this negativity gone, you have more room for positive, productive thoughts about your creativity.

Another notion that can inhibit creativity is the belief that the process is a mystery, reserved for the gifted few and occurring in some realm beyond the reach of most. On the contrary, the ability to be creative comes with *every* healthy brain. As you use your creativity, you demystify the process and bring it into the realm of your everyday life. This next activity will help.

With your personal definition, make a public declaration of yourself as a creative individual. Go to a mirror and, looking yourself in the eyes, declare out loud, "I am a creative person. I enjoy being creative in many ways." Say it several times, paying attention to how you feel about hearing this affirmation. Sometimes the words are immediately comfortable. Sometimes they feel like a new pair of shoes that fit but need to be broken in. And sometimes the words feel distant, foreign.

Note your voice pitch as you make your declaration. Is it higher than usual? If so, you may be having trouble believing what you're saying. Repeat the two statements, keeping your pitch normal or even slightly lower than normal. Now how do you feel?

Affirmations need to be tied to strong, positive feelings to be effective. Breathe deeply and allow yourself to feel power and strength while saying, "I am a creative person." Feel the excitement and joy in declaring, "I enjoy being creative in many ways." Think of a moment in your life when you were creative and relive the empowering feelings you had at the time. Let those feelings move through your body. Tie as many positive emotions as you can to these affirmations.

Meet yourself eye-to-eye in the mirror once again. Breathing deeply and keeping your voice solid, reaffirm, "I am a creative person. I enjoy being creative in many ways." Allow feelings like joy, power, and enthusiasm to move through you. Hear and feel the truth of these words.

While tuning up your awareness of yourself as a creative being, think about what other women say when describing their sense of being creative. A homemaker states, "I feel *sooo* good. It's such a natural high." A journalist writes, "There is an enormous, almost physical, sense of satisfaction. A glow." Another writer has similar body sensations. "Physically I may feel shivers run down my spine. My cheeks flush. The butterflies that live in my tummy clap." A software and instructional designer says, "There's a clean, crystal-clear satisfaction." What sensations are connected to your feelings of being creative?

The Creative Lifestyle

I often talk about living a creative lifestyle as being the ultimate purpose for creativity. This lifestyle continually integrates new learning into behavior, changing and maturing a woman in the process. Problems become challenges to creativity. A dilemma is only the start of an exciting adventure. The creator is truly alive. Every time you use an activity from this book to develop your creativity, you reinforce your creative lifestyle. You enhance in yourself the traits of a creative individual.

Creative people tend to possess many positive qualities. Some of these qualities are:

- Ability to get along with others
- Ability to plan
- Capacity to recognize and solve problems
- Independence
- Ability to see the whole picture
- A sense of humor
- A high degree of honesty
- A sense of social responsibility
- A desire to make positive contributions to the world.

The following activity is designed to help you realize how many of these qualities are already a part of you.

Think of the creative people you know. Write their names on a sheet of paper, leaving lots of room between each name. Now list the creative behaviors or qualities you have observed in these people. Which of these traits do you have? Make a list. Or have someone who knows you very well make this list about you. Which qualities would you like to uncover or enhance in yourself? Make a list of these, too.

Now choose one quality or behavior from your last list. Or you may want to simply use the word *creative*. Write the word on ten or so notecards, all the same color. Place these cards where you'll see them regularly—the bathroom mirror, refrigerator, dashboard, a desk drawer you open often, beside your bed. Look at the word on the card throughout the day, especially just before you fall asleep and first thing in the morning. As you see the word, simply allow yourself to be aware of it, then resume your usual activities. You don't have to work at this. Simply surround yourself with reminders of the quality you want to strengthen in yourself.

Every time you exhibit the desired behavior, congratulate yourself. Write a word or two about it on one of the cards so they begin to fill with tangible evidence of your progress. When you feel confident with this new behavior, replace its cards with another quality written on cards of a different color. Work on only one trait at a time, giving yourself several weeks with each. Using a distinctive color with each quality will help you associate that color with the behavior, regardless of where you see the color.

Celebrate to mark the changing of the cards. Plan a dinner at your favorite restaurant, buy yourself something a bit unusual, or take a day trip to your favorite outdoor place.

You've taken a significant step, and by rewarding your progress, you are honoring yourself—honoring your creativity.

The Holistic Process: Its Praises and Pitfalls

I'm writing a book. Do I see this book idea by idea, or even section by section? Not really. I see the whole thing—not the details, but all the sections and ideas together at once. Right now, I experience this book holistically. But if I write it holistically, you'll probably have a difficult time understanding my messages. My ideas may seem scattered and unconnected. So, I write about one main idea at a time, fitting all my thoughts together as I progress.

This is typical of women's holistic thinking and creating processes. We see the whole first, then break out the details. Men tend to do the opposite. They use linear thinking, seeing the details first, then fitting those together to form the whole. Linear thinking is what we learned in school as "logical thinking." We were told any other process was illogical and, therefore, no good. Holistic thinking is natural for most women, while linear thinking is natural for most men—although both sexes are certainly capable of using each type. Since Nature never creates waste, holistic and linear thinking exist to balance each other. One is not better than the other. Let's take a closer look at these thinking styles.

Linear Thinking

The linear thinking process basically goes like this: In order to get to D, you must start with A. Of course, A must be true. From A you can move to B, which also must be true. The next step is to C, which is based on both A and B and also must be true. From C you can arrive at D, confident it is true because all your previous steps are true. At least you hope they are. Opposites cannot coexist in this structure; if one statement were true and another false, the latter would need to be eliminated. So linear thinking reduces information down to accepted truths and eliminates everything else.

$$A \rightarrow B \rightarrow C \rightarrow D$$

Linear thinking has many uses: keeping accurate financial records, giving and understanding directions, organizing a speech or book. A linear agenda can keep a meeting focused and on task. Unfortunately, linear thinking has been overemphasized as the *only* way. Used exclusively, it results in tunneled, noncreative thinking. When applied to problem-solving, for example, linear thinking can lead to solutions that merely cause more problems because it provides no means to see the ramifications of the answers. For instance, the linear process resulted in "solving" traffic congestion in many cities by building freeways, which, in turn, have become more congested with traffic, creating a bigger problem. The solution becomes a problem.

Holistic Thinking

In contrast, the holistic process enables you to see the whole picture at once, then sort out the details. To arrive at D using a holistic process, you might begin with X. From X you can hop to M, then slide to G, and then jump to D. You can start anywhere—even with D—and move in any direction. All information can be included, even seeming opposites. With holistic thinking, opposites are often seen as different aspects of the same phenomenon. Black and white are simply shades of gray. The "truth" of some piece of information is determined by how well it fits into the whole picture. Holistic thinking is inherently creative.

An inclusive process, holistic thinking encourages the joining of previously unrelated pieces of information because it allows all possibilities to coexist. This is an important part of the creative process. If you must gather material about an issue, a holistic approach enables you to collect a great deal of data and decide later what's the most important. This way, you avoid eliminating potentially valuable information prematurely. Using a holistic process, you can anticipate implications of proposed solutions and be more likely to choose one that really answers the problem.

To someone whose primary thinking style is linear, holistic thinking can be confusing, offering too many alternatives. People who use only linear thinking are generally impatient with the holistic process, accusing it of being scattered and time-consuming. In fact, the holistic approach is very efficient because it can offer solutions that solve the problem rather than cause more problems.

Thinking Holistically in a Linear World

Conflicts arise frequently for women using holistic thinking in a world where linear thinking predominates. A participant in one of my seminars described a common situation. She and a male co-worker were assigned to the task of gathering information about a problem, agreeing on a solution, and presenting their answer to their peers and supervisor. Her description of the experience went something like this:

" *I* went into our first meeting full of enthusiasm. I had all kinds of ideas about the problem and where we could get a bunch of information. I was set to do all sorts of things. But shortly after I started describing what I wanted to do, I could tell he was lost. He just sort of stared at me. He cut me off to say we should look at this and this and this. He seemed to know exactly what he wanted to do and how he would do it. And he dismissed my approach and my ideas. He wanted the task to be kept simple, or so he said. It seemed to me that if we approached the problem his way, we would miss the whole point. But his attitude toward my approach was so obviously negative, and I felt so insecure, I didn't try to convince him. Finally, we agreed to work separately.

"We had a follow-up meeting about a week later. The whole tone was different. He had his information, I had mine, and we could go from there. But I felt odd about the first meeting. I didn't understand what happened. And I know there have been times in my life, when I was less sure of myself, when I would have given up on my approach and copied his. Now I understand we were simply using our different styles. In the end we worked everything out, but we each had to do it our own way. "

Women are told from the time we start school that linear thinking is the only acceptable style. Our natural holistic process is dismissed, with many unfortunate results:

- Poor self-image
- An uneasy sense that we don't deserve our accomplishments
- Distrust of our innate processes
- A brittle approach to problem-solving and even to life in general.

If we believe that our innate thinking process is no good, self-esteem is damaged. As a result, many women decide they are not intelligent. For example, I know one successful writer who says that she's not very smart. She is a holistic thinker who never could grasp linear thinking. So in spite of the abundant evidence that her special intelligence enables her to put universal themes into enjoyable, award-winning books, she still tells me that she's not intelligent. She is fortunate that this notion hasn't interfered with her talent and creativity. Too often, a negative self-concept damages the entire personality.

One choice many of us made in first or second grade was to mask our natural holistic thinking in favor of the predominant linear style. In other words, we kept our holistic process alive by secretly using it, but then we translated the results into a linear format for others to see. While ultimately this survival mechanism is healthy in that we retained our natural process while learning the other, it, too, can result in some psychological damage.

For example, all through school, I did math backward. I'd look at a problem, let it go "out of focus" (my way of describing the diffused logic of the holistic process), and let my mind work out the answer. Then I worked backward from the answer to see how I got there. Once I arrived at the beginning, I could present my solution in a linear way. I did this in the same amount of time it seemed to take my classmates to work the problem linearly. I thought I was the only person in the class using this unorthodox approach. I've learned since that most female students were doing the same! But at the time, none of us ever talked about it. And most of us thought somehow we were "cheating" because we weren't using the method described by teachers as being "correct." When I describe this experience to a group of women, I see most heads nod in agreement. Does it bring back any memories for you?

This feeling of cheating can remain part of a woman's concept of her learning throughout her life. No matter what her accomplishments, she knows she's using a method other than the accepted one. Therefore, she assumes somehow she's inferior to everyone else who uses the predominant linear approach. I've met women with doctorates and women in upper-management positions who still feel this sense of inferiority. In spite of their success, they doubt their holistic approach as a valid thinking and creating style because they learned as children that it was wrong. The challenge is to appreciate how flexible this thinking is.

Another way of coping for many female six- and seven-year-olds is to repress, or hold back, the holistic thinking process altogether. A young girl quickly learns that male behaviors, including linear thinking, are rewarded in this society. But by adopting the linear style and refusing to acknowledge any other, she can become very rigid in her thinking, seeing only a single way to do things. Her linear thinking becomes especially tunneled. When confronted with a new approach, she will resist, finding as many flaws as she can. Even if she cannot find fault in the new way, she will simply refuse to try it. Insisting the old method has always worked, she asks, "Why change?"—a question she doesn't want answered.

I have seen many women become angry when they realize this conflict as adults. Sometimes the anger is directed at society, sometimes at themselves. If you do become angry, be forgiving. You were very young when you made your choices. And regardless of your decision then, you can change now. We must all learn to honor ourselves for our abilities and to balance linear and holistic thinking. As we make these changes within ourselves, we change society.

Striking a Balance

Holistic and linear thinking complement each other. Total reliance on linear thinking results in the narrow solutions that have caused our society more problems. And using holistic thinking exclusively has pitfalls, too.

Suppose you have to prepare for a problem-solving session at work. You would probably begin by gathering as much information as possible to understand the issue. A holistic approach is excellent here because it enables you to see the whole issue. The more you see, the more you will include and the better chance you have of folding in information vital to the ultimate solution. But herein lies the trap: Because you want to know as much as possible, you may want to continue gathering data rather than begin the problem-solving. As a result, you will be ill-prepared for the meeting, looking indecisive and lacking focus. Linear thinkers will quickly become impatient with what they see as a rambling, directionless presentation. Your argument of needing more time to compile information will carry little weight. What a flop!

So how do you do both, thinking holistically and linearly at the same time? Simple. Before you start to gather information, set a deadline. Stick to that decision, even if you firmly believe you could use a few more hours, another day, or one more week. You may have to mentally grit your teeth to honor your deadline, but we can never know all there is to know about any subject. What we *can* hope to accomplish is knowing the most important, relevant information. When you have stopped accumulating data holistically, you can then organize your information using linear thinking. The most pertinent data can be put together in a step-by-step pattern which is easily understood by others.

Applying a combination of holistic and linear thinking to any project will make the outcome much stronger and more complete than using only one style because it allows you to draw on the strengths in both approaches. The higher you progress in management in any setting, the more you need the ability to see both the big picture and the details.

The Outline Doesn't Have to Happen First

Here's a common classroom scene: Every time we had to write a long paper, usually beginning in about the ninth grade, we heard, "Outline first!" Most of us adapted the same way to this dilemma—write the paper first, *then* construct the outline. This worked until we had teachers who wanted to approve the outline before we began writing the paper. Or the assignment length became longer and the research more complex, so writing the entire paper before we got outline approval became increasingly difficult. Besides, many of us knew deep inside we were "cheating" because we weren't following the prescribed process.

As most women experience it, the "outline first" dilemma sets up a conflict between linear and holistic approaches. The outline is a linear approach which reduces information to accepted facts, while writing the paper first is a holistic approach which allows for including all related data. As with similar conflicts, the impact on women's creativity has generally been negative. Unfortunately, as we struggled to use a linear approach instead of our natural, holistic style, many of us concluded that we could not write or even that we were stupid. Trust in our innate holistic process eroded as a result of this conflict. Women who used the holistic process first, then the linear, may have felt that they were inferior because they weren't using the accepted method.

Many women still accept this notion and approach every writing endeavor (or speaking, since speeches begin with writing) as if it's a classroom assignment requiring outline approval.

This needless damage to women's creativity and self-esteem can be stopped. Holistic and linear methods can be combined to maximize creativity while enabling the creator to communicate her thoughts and ideas clearly. When a holistic approach is used first to generate ideas, all possibilities are considered, even if they cannot all be handled within one paper or speech. Later, the ideas can be sorted to choose the strongest, most important concepts. The resulting presentation can be easily communicated in a traditional linear format. The following activity is designed to help accomplish a holistic/linear balance.

≈

An effective technique for coping with the "outline first" dilemma is to write each main idea, along with assorted thoughts about it, on a separate note card. (I like to use large, 5″ by 8″ cards since they accommodate a great deal of information.) The supporting thoughts can be written in any order, preferably short phrases rather than sentences. Make sure to record all of your ideas. Organization and proper phrasing can happen later. Carry your note cards with you, so when a creative thought strikes in some unlikely spot—such as in the middle of a traffic jam—you can jot it down. I even know a scuba diver who keeps her waterproof slate and pencil in the shower to catch good ideas for her business while showering!

Once all of your ideas are on notecards, you can begin organizing your thoughts. Clear your desk and lay out the cards so you can see all of them at once. Then shuffle and reshuffle until you find the strongest flow of ideas. You may find that some ideas can be combined with others or that some can be eliminated altogether. Or you may discover some areas that need more research but have to be set aside because there's no time left before your deadline. Eventually an organization for your ideas will begin to reveal itself and, at that point, you can begin to actually write the paper or speech. If you need a written outline, you can lift it from the cards.

You might find the organization process more stimulating if you do it away from your usual workplace. Take your cards to a park or to your favorite restaurant. Throw them on the floor and sit down, in your best childlike fashion, and sort. The idea is to give yourself a fresh perspective on your thoughts.

One Final Note

Even though we can understand the importance of using both holistic and linear methods appropriately, our education system perpetuates the conflict between them. Instead of teaching students how to use both thinking styles to complement each other, the "outline first" approach still reigns. As you learn to balance yourself and to live creatively, you may encourage those around you to do likewise. But don't expect the system to begin encouraging creativity immediately. Instead, be responsible for teaching your children and circle of associates these techniques as you learn them. Encourage others to join in the fun! Perhaps if we all touch one or two people, the system *will* eventually change.

$\mathcal{F}$inishing What You Start

Women are fascinated by how we do things. Men are fascinated with what they do. Why? Many years ago, psychologist Abraham Maslow observed that women are *process-oriented,* while men are *product-oriented.*[1] These two distinct orientations result in differing perspectives of creativity. Most women are interested in the experience of creating. If we feel any dissatisfaction around our creativity, our natural inclination is to examine what we're doing and how. To improve the product we will first enhance the process. Men, on the other hand, tend to focus on the product of their creativity rather than on what they went through to produce it. They center attention on tangible results to make improvements. Both perspectives have equal validity.

Our fascination with process—the *how* part—can cause us a major problem: not finishing the *what* part. As a creative endeavor concludes, women can lose interest in the result. Our attention is on the process, which is completed before the product. Just prior to finishing the work, our interest may shift to the next project—and its new process. When this happens, we may drop the venture we've been working on, leaving the product unfinished, in order to move to the next, more absorbing process . . . uh, I mean project. In other words, we may not always finish what we start.

In many of us the process orientation is so strong that we need to develop tremendous self-discipline to stay with a project through completion. In fact, creative work takes more self-discipline than any other endeavor. Ideally, motivation to finish creative tasks originates from an interest in *both* the process *and* the product. Self-discipline is healthiest when it arises naturally from a desire to give form to creative efforts.

A study conducted several years ago by Dr. Jean Houston provides some insight into this ambition.[2] Houston wanted to know what makes a genius a genius. Among other attributes, she learned that geniuses finish what they start. They also plan their creative efforts by using imagery before beginning a project. In other words, they see or imagine themselves solving a problem several different ways, then they choose the best way. The use of imagery mobilizes a natural drive to complete the task, then they do it. In follow-up studies involving average people, Houston discovered people are more likely to finish what they start if they image themselves completing the work before they actually begin.

Using this information, you can learn to give yourself the best chance for finishing the creative projects you start. You can image by yourself, almost anywhere—in your office, at home, in an airplane. Try this next activity and see.

~~~

Begin by closing your eyes to block out external distractions. Focus your attention on your breathing for a few minutes. Follow the breath in with your awareness, then follow it out. Let your attention on your breathing help you to concentrate. Now see yourself at the start of a project, making necessary preparations. You might see and hear yourself talking with others involved. You might be alone at your computer or easel or desk.

Involve as many senses as you can throughout this activity. Smell the room you're in; hear what you might be saying; feel the texture of the canvas or your desktop;

taste the coffee or soda or snack you usually enjoy while working; look at your surroundings and notice details.

Continue to image yourself moving through the project, doing all the things necessary to accomplish the task. See the finished product. Touch it, smell it, taste it, hear it. Make it as real as you can. If the product is intangible, you can still see or hear or otherwise sense the results of your efforts. For example, creating a more positive work atmosphere can be experienced by feeling a deep sense of inner satisfaction as you see co-workers behaving more harmoniously.

The more vividly you can image the results of your creative efforts before you begin creating them, the more likely you'll be to complete what you start. Once you thoroughly experience imaging the process and its product, you're ready to begin actual work. Imagining the process with the product activates your enthusiasm and inner drive to complete the project. You may still feel your interest waning just before you conclude the work, but you will be prepared to stay with it and finish. Try it the next time you start a project and see if it makes a difference!

$\mathcal{L}$earning to Change Reality

The art of changing reality forms a vital part of the holistic, creative process. The challenge in the creative act involves synthesizing ideas, feelings, or images into new forms. If we accept the status quo, never questioning "facts," new forms will not be created. But if we use holistic thinking, we encourage opposites to coexist. We stimulate a different perspective of the relationship among concepts. Rightness or wrongness is suspended—at least temporarily—so all possibilities can be considered. The creative individual using holistic thinking in this way is shifting reality by rejecting the accepted relationship among ideas and searching for an association that previously never existed.

To be creative, we often must overcome our education which tells us what we believe to be true. In 1956, Patsy Sherman, a research chemist for 3M, managed to overcome her beliefs about what was true when she accidentally spilled a chemical she was working with onto her tennis shoes.[1] As she was trying to clean the substance off, she began noticing its effect on her shoes. Suspending her knowledge of the chemical's original purpose, Sherman observed it harden into a coating that protected the shoe from picking up dirt. And that's how Scotchgard was discovered.

One of the greatest inventors of our century, Bill Lear, was long-practiced at creative questioning of the status quo.[2] For example, he was the first to figure out how to make a radio small enough to fit into a car—at a time when college students were being taught that a radio this small was impossible to manufacture. Lear didn't know he couldn't do it, so he did it. And in the process, he reconceptualized scientific thought of the day.

A healthy rejection of reality can be applied effectively to many situations that call for creative thinking. One client of mine relayed her frustration with a common predicament:

> " *I* was in a meeting with other department heads. One of them, I'll call her Kathy, had a problem which required immediate resolution. Our manager asked us to help so we all began generating ideas. But Kathy rejected every one of them. She's usually very creative so her attitude surprised me. She kept saying, 'You just don't understand. That idea won't work. I need to solve this by myself.' The more we tried to help her, the more narrow she became. Instead of trying to get her to consider our suggestions, our boss allowed Kathy to become more and more rigid. Ultimately, the solution she decided on caused problems for some other departments. It wasn't up to her usual level of creativity. What could I have done? "

I made two suggestions to my client about this situation. First, she needed to realize that creativity often breaks down under stress. My client described Kathy as a strong, independent person who was clearly feeling a lot of pressure. When she felt more stress, she naturally retreated into her independence, her status quo. As a result, she rejected everyone's suggestions and, at the same time, became increasingly rigid. Trying to force a person in this dilemma to become more open often has the reverse effect—they cling harder to the familiar.

Second, I suggested to my client that she meet with her boss to discuss ways to stimulate more creativity in their meetings. Her emphasis had to be on problem-solving and not on the personalities involved. She also had to make tangible suggestions for how to improve the process. For example, to stimulate a more creative atmosphere, the group might change the reality about a proposed solution by considering it a completed success. Taking this perspective, the focus for the group becomes, "How did we make this successful?" rather than, "What will we do?" Everyone considers the project a done deal. The idea can then be examined in its totality, including implementation and outcome. Precise details don't need to be worked out for every proposal, just enough so the benefits, if any, are apparent. Sometimes part of an idea proves workable or gives rise to better solutions that wouldn't have been discovered without thoroughly examining the original suggestion.

Another way to stimulate more creativity is to ask the group to suspend reality by assuming that any given suggestion will solve the problem. Now the question becomes, "How can we make this work?" Putting a time limit of, say, five minutes for considering each suggestion helps keep the group moving toward a viable solution. As with the previous approach, the group may discover a workable resolution from combining the best aspects of several proposals.

Both of these tactics take the focus away from the stress of an imminent deadline, shifting it to developing a creative resolution to the issue. Bear in mind, though, that they also require strong leadership to keep the group moving forward. One person who clings rigidly to the status quo can keep the whole group at a standstill. But once everyone begins to play with reality, shifting and changing it to see what might happen, creative opportunities abound.

When was the last time you suspended what you "knew to be true" so that new possibilities could arise? If it's been a while, I invite you to find some way today to change reality in search of the creative.

Understanding Your Feminine Nature

Mysterious . . . elusive . . . like trying to catch a handful of fog: so the feminine is often described. But when we begin talking about this quality, attempting to define it in tangible ways, we immediately lose its essence. Yet the feminine is the source of our creative energy, so we need to understand it. But how?

All of us, women and men, have both a feminine and a masculine aspect, with distinct characteristics which influence our behavior. The feminine in women expresses itself differently from the way it manifests in men, just as the masculine in men shows itself differently from the way it does in women. Because we're focusing on our creativity, we'll examine the feminine in women. The qualities we're concentrating on have nothing to do with being "feminine" as defined by our society. So dump the images of frilly dresses, patent-leather shoes, and holding a teacup a certain way.

One excellent way to understand the feminine is by looking at mythology, the ancient stories of gods and goddesses. The late Joseph Campbell, a leading mythology expert, described myths as coming from the "unfiltered unconscious." In other words, mythical goddesses and gods and their stories originate in the human unconscious; their conduct is seen in our behavior. So when we examine goddess behavior, we're also gaining insight into our own feminine nature, into our creativity.

Within mythology sharp distinctions exist between the Greek and Roman myths most of us are familiar with and the earlier pre-Greek stories of the goddesses that arose from oral cultures. In relating these two versions to our behavior, the more familiar goddesses are often depicted as negative and male-defined.[1, 2] The original goddesses, on the other hand, are portrayed as strong, self-defined individuals who give insight into the richness of the feminine.[3] These myths also provide a clearer understanding of the relationship between the feminine and creativity.

We're going to look at seven goddesses, comparing their Greek and pre-Greek versions and drawing parallels between their behaviors and those of modern women. They may remind you of yourself or of women you know. Pay attention to these similarities—they are an important source of creative strength.

Hera

In Greek mythology Hera is the possessive, jealous wife of Zeus; she is a woman who takes revenge upon her husband's many mistresses. Originally, however, she was the Supreme Earth Goddess, embodying a dignified and self-assured feminine. In her role as Goddess of Marriage, she presides over the sacred marriage of the lunar cow and solar bull. Hera demonstrates the feminine ability to nurture relationships. Does she sound familiar?

Aphrodite

Aphrodite is commonly known as the Goddess of Love, bringing joy to all living creatures. While the Greeks often portrayed her as manipulative and vain, the earlier mythology depicts her as independent and eternally beautiful. She wanders the countryside bringing joy and love to all creatures. She represents the desire held by many creative women to give something loving and beautiful to the world. Like Hera, Aphrodite exhibits the feminine ability to nourish relationships. Who do you know who has these qualities?

Demeter and Persephone

As mother and daughter, Demeter and Persephone are earth goddesses with important ties to Nature. Demeter is Mother Earth, creating life itself. Persephone is both the Goddess of Spring and the Queen of the Underworld. As such, she brings forth new life every spring and allows it to wither and die in fall and winter. Women who identify with these goddesses usually have the proverbial green thumb. Gardening or simply being outdoors are important ways for them to relax and re-energize.

A distinct contrast exists between the pre-classical and Greek/Roman patriarchal versions of Persephone's descent into the land of the dead. The Greeks portray her as flighty, easily captured, and forced underground by Hades, Lord of the Underworld. She becomes depressed, refusing to eat. Demeter also responds to this crisis with depression, withholding her abundance from Earth. Nothing grows. Hades is finally persuaded to release Persephone, but first he convinces her to eat a pomegranate seed. This act binds her to return to the underworld.

While this story offers an explanation of the seasons, it also shows us a weak feminine embodied in someone who is vulnerable to depression and forced into the depths (underworld) by a domineering masculine. Certainly many women experience the truth of cycling powerlessly into and out of depressions, but they do not have to be trapped by this phenomenon.

In the pre-classical myth of Persephone as the Queen of the Underworld, her journey into the depths is motivated by her instinctive knowing that it is something she must do. She descends willingly into the underworld, where she performs a ritual of receiving and renewing the dead. She ascends at the appropriate time, a changed woman who brings forth new life.

We can see several important aspects of the feminine in these goddesses. First, Persephone shows us the natural inclination to travel into the inner self while trusting our basic instincts. Our creative process often involves an inward journey which changes us. As we express our creativity, we must frequently rely on our instincts to trust our process and give us the courage to develop something new.

Demeter and Persephone also illustrate the close ties between the feminine and Nature. In Nature all events are interrelated; life and death are one. The feminine experiences life just as Nature does—one event affects all other events in a never-ending cycle, a holistic interaction with life. Our natural leaning toward holistic thinking comes, at least in part, from our feminine nature.

Hestia

One of the least-known and most-unappreciated goddesses in mythology is Hestia. While no specific mention of her can be found in the early oral mythology, she was important to the daily lives of the Greeks. As Goddess of the Hearth, Hestia makes a house a home. Newborns were carried around her fires before being accepted into the family. Jungian psychologist Esther Harding attributes the existence of a home to the particular creative genius of women.[4] The intangible feeling sensed in a home, classroom, or office has been created through this feminine quality. The feminine creates the atmosphere in which relationships can be nurtured. You may have expressed this ability within the last twenty-four hours.

Athena

In contrast to Hestia, Athena is well-known. The Greeks identified her as Goddess of Defensive War, born out of Zeus's head and fully armored. But prior to this version, Athena possessed many peaceful duties. She nurtured arts and crafts, teaching women to spin, weave, and make pottery. As Goddess of Wisdom, Athena gave women the spiral, symbolic of our holistic thinking and creative processes. This strong goddess personifies a highly creative yet practical feminine prepared to protect that creativity in battle if necessary. These days, Athena is often found in the business world, as is her sister, Artemis.

Artemis

The changes imposed by the Greeks upon Artemis weren't as radical as those suffered by other goddesses. In the earlier myths she is Goddess of Untamed Nature. The Greeks made her patron of hunters. Artemis shows us a complex feminine containing many paradoxes. She is connected with forests, the hunt, and the moon. This association with the moon and its rhythmic phases symbolizes the ever-changing, cyclic nature of the feminine. Within her earthly realm Artemis protects equally the hunter who must kill for food and the hunted whose young must survive to adulthood. What looks like conflict on the surface is actually different aspects of the same phenomenon. Do these paradoxes feel familiar to you in your life?

Exhibiting both compassion and dispassion, Artemis assists women in childbirth while bringing a painless death to those who don't survive the birth. Artemis unveils a feminine filled with seeming opposites reconciled as part of the cycles of Nature. Generally depicted carrying a bow and arrows, Artemis always hits the bull's-eye. This naturally goal-oriented goddess represents that part of the feminine enabling us to accomplish whatever we choose.

Summary and Activity

This brief look at goddesses yields many elements vital to an understanding of the feminine and women's creativity.

See
The Holistic Process: Its Praises and Pitfalls
p. 19

- We have strong ties to Nature along with a holistic perspective, crucial in creativity. ◀
- The feminine possesses an inherent ability with relationships—nurturing them into being and creating the environment for their healthy survival. (But because relationships are intangible, the creativity involved is frequently overlooked.)
- By following our instincts we can reach the feminine wisdom residing in our depths.
- Contradictions seem to exist within the feminine as parts of the same cycle. Creative forms can arise from our search for similarities among what looks like opposites.

As we nurture our feminine aspect, we also nourish our creativity. The following activities are designed to help you become more intimate with your feminine nature.

Because the feminine and Nature are interconnected, the best place to stimulate the feminine within yourself is outdoors. If you can, go outside right now. Try closing your eyes and listening to sounds. Allow Nature's songs to envelop you. Feel the breeze on your skin. Relax, becoming one with Nature's breath so you can't tell where your skin leaves off and the breeze begins.

Or watch a bird riding air currents. Project yourself into the bird. Feel the gentle rise and fall as you and the bird and the air are one. How's the view from up there? Can you see yourself as the bird sees you?

As you become one with Nature, avoid labeling. A name will only separate you from the thing being labeled. It's enough to say, "What a beautiful tree" or "That's a lovely song that bird is singing." The kind of tree or species of bird is unimportant.

If you plan this activity for as little as ten to fifteen minutes as part of your daily routine, you're more likely to follow through. Early in the morning before the day's activities begin is good for some. Others prefer incorporating Nature with lunch. If you juggle both a career outside the home and a family, try spending time outdoors as soon as you return home from work. You may have to train your family to respect this time and leave you alone, but with persistence you can engage others' cooperation. Or encourage them to join you! We're all more pleasant to be around after releasing the day's tensions. If getting outdoors is difficult for you or the weather is inhospitable, a windowpane doesn't need to be a barrier.

Each time you lose your sense of self by becoming at one with Nature, you are nurturing your feminine and your creativity, giving rise to the self-defined goddess within.

Take some time now to review each of the seven goddesses we just discussed. You might want to go outdoors for this. Do you feel especially drawn to one? Or does one of the goddesses feel drawn to you? Invite her to reveal herself and to speak with you. What do you ask her? How does she respond? You may be establishing the beginning of an ongoing relationship that will nurture your creativity. You might ask her how you can contact her when you need her assistance. Listen carefully to what your goddess tells you.

Get a designated goddess-conversation notebook to record your conversations in writing. Can you draw a picture of her?

Goddesses are often very insistent and direct in their support of our endeavors. Make time for your goddess on a regular basis and she will become one of your best friends. You may find that different goddesses come to you as your needs vary. Welcome them.

Put this book aside right now. Give yourself the time and space to make these important connections.

Part Two

Developing
Your Unique Process

$\mathcal{K}$eep It Private—
For a While

The Feeling Connection

We're exploring an intimate relationship in this book—the one between us and our creativity. Our creations result from combining our innermost feelings with an idea or issue or emotion. So throughout the creative process, we're completely identified with what we are doing and how we're doing it. Artist Judy Chicago once explained, "The canvas was like my own skin; I was the painting and the painting was me."[1] This total connection is typical of women's creativity.

Because our feelings are tied to our products, some psychologists warn we shouldn't go public with our creative works. They say that as we bring forth our books, paintings, solutions to business problems, or other creative endeavors, we open up these works to criticism. Our emotional selves as expressed in these ventures are also vulnerable to the same harsh treatment. And because emotional development is inhibited in an environment of criticism, our psychological growth can be thwarted. Therefore, these psychologists suggest that we need to keep our creative works private and away from critical analysis rather than attempt to gain societal recognition for them. Or so their argument goes.

I believe, however, that this contention makes us seem weak in our creativity, potentially damaged by critics who scrutinize the apparently fragile results of our creative process. In fact, just the opposite is true. The infusion of inner feelings into our creative products forms one of our major strengths. These feelings impart depth and power to our creative works.

A few years ago, Anna Quindlen, Pulitzer-prizewinning columnist and best-selling novelist, had this to say about her reliance on emotions in her writing:

> *Do I buy into the idea that the intellect always tells the truth and the emotions are somehow second-rate and suspect? I think that's a scam to devalue women's voices. Because historically we've tended to be in touch with the emotional tenor of our lives, somehow it turns out the emotions aren't really very valuable at all [and] what we really should be concentrating on is the intellect. No. I think we should strike a nice healthy balance between the two.* [2]

Our process has a built-in protective mechanism overlooked by those who want us to keep our creative expressions private: just as we totally identify with our creations while they are in process, we *dis*identify with them upon completion. In other words, when we follow our process to the point of creating a satisfying product, we become detached from the outcome and the feelings entwined in it just before it's finished. This occurs as a natural part of women's total creative process.

This phenomenon of detachment is partially connected to our process orientation. Prior to completing a creative work, we tend to become bored, losing interest because the process is finished; we want to move on to the next creative effort. ◀ This disinterest begins the detachment which completes itself as we finish the work, making it possible for us to take our creative endeavors public without being concerned

See
Finishing What You Start
p. 31

that criticism may thwart our growth. Consider these two artists' experiences.

The Painter

“Once I've finished a painting and then later go back into my studio to sign it, I feel as if I didn't paint it. It feels very separate from me. When I look at my work in a show, I often feel as if I'm viewing someone else's paintings. As far as criticism and reviews of my work are concerned, I find them interesting. It's nice when I can learn something, but I'm never emotionally crushed or stymied by it. But certainly when I'm making my art, I am totally identified with it. It really does contain my innermost feelings at that moment.”

The Writer

“When I'm writing, I'm putting myself into the book. It's an expression of who I am. But once it's finished and I get the completed version from the publisher, I look at it as if someone else had written it. Critics don't bother me. I've never felt stifled by criticism.”

The Benefits

These accomplished women have an attitude that welcomes learning something from critics' feedback. If we never put our works into the public arena, we'll never have the benefits that can come from constructive criticism.

Every time we allow our creativity to run its full course, we are nurturing the strength that accompanies growth. When we combine ideas or feelings with an emotion as we bring forth a new creation, we're experiencing our inner selves from a different perspective. Detaching from that experience to move to the next creative endeavor enables us to open ourselves to a new encounter with ideas and feelings. We are inviting further growth. The feelings embodied in a painting created six months ago aren't the feelings we experience today. We have moved to a new level on our inner spiral, to a new sense of self-awareness, and to a stronger experience of our power.

Stop right now and recall a time when you felt especially creative. Can you tap into the feelings of inner strength, power, and joy which accompanied that experience? Settle into those feelings, letting them move through your entire body. Own them as part of your rightful inheritance.

The Challenge

Nature provides women with a creative process which nurtures this kind of emotional maturation. But the process has to be followed through to completion for the detachment to happen. If we expose our creative ideas too soon, the feelings involved can be vulnerable to criticism. Even a well-intended comment can squash an idea if we are too attached to the feelings connected with it.

When we are working at our leisure, we can give ourselves the time we need to become dispassionate about our creations. But working under an imposed deadline can cause a problem. If we're putting our best creative effort into arriving at an effective solution to a problem and we don't have enough time to detach from the feelings involved, we may be setting ourselves up for difficulty when we present the idea. Any criticism made against the idea may be taken personally and we may become defensive.

The part of the feminine portrayed by Athena—who is ready to vigorously defend creative works—can become so aroused that we refuse to listen to constructive suggestions. ◄ We may feel protective of our efforts and become rigidly entrenched. When a woman in this situation happens to be the boss, she'll fail to elicit the support of her employees in the problem-solving process. When she is the employee, her boss and peers may see her as inflexible and unable to take constructive criticism.

See
Understanding Your Feminine Nature
p. 39

The Solution

Finding ourselves in such a situation may call for making a choice. One approach to protect your creativity may be remaining silent rather than prematurely proposing a solution. Feeling emotionally trampled by criticism heard too soon can discourage you from exercising your creativity in the future. Or you can speed up the detachment process by using the following suggestions.

The next time you're working on a project, write out your proposed solution, then list as many objections to it as you can generate. Objections might include statements like:

- We tried that before. It didn't work.
- The boss will never accept your idea.
- This will take too much time.
- It will cost too much money.
- Your idea is too simple; it won't work.

Now read your entire list out loud, perhaps even imagining who might be saying each objection. If you feel yourself becoming defensive, breathe deeply to help eliminate this sense of defensiveness. As you feel protective feelings coming up, take deep breaths, then imagine you're releasing the stifling feelings with the expelled breath. Keep doing this until you can consider the objection without feeling on guard.

Now discuss your idea with a co-worker whose opinions you value. Listen to any criticisms offered, using deep breathing to keep yourself from becoming defensive.

By examining as many objections to your solution as you can generate, you'll make your creative work stronger and you will also be better prepared to answer criticisms objectively. After you've made these efforts to detach, you can decide whether you're prepared to present your solution in a more public way.

At times, we can use our intimate involvement with our creative endeavors to keep them seemingly forever in process. An analogy women often use when describing their creative process is that it is like giving birth. The creative experience can be one of bringing forth a new life from deep within ourselves. So, our relationship to our creative work can be similar to feelings we would have for a child. And sometimes we hesitate to "let the child grow up," not allowing our creative process to complete itself to the point where we detach from our involved feelings. As long as we remain so attached, our feelings are vulnerable.

More than one potential writer has said to me that she can't bear the thought of sending her manuscript to an agent or a publisher because of the anticipated brutal criticism which might follow. They often deliberately forestall completing a work by continually working and reworking the book, whether or not it's improved by those efforts. I know an artist who worked for over five years on the same painting, adding detail after detail. When I questioned her about the subject matter, she explained that it was a favorite place from her otherwise unhappy childhood. Eventually she realized she feared that finishing the work would mean the end of her pleasant memories.

This attitude keeps us stuck—we'll never move to the next creative project or climb to the next level of our growth spiral. The development of our creative process is paralyzed. By finishing creative works and, if appropriate, sharing them with trusted friends, we can stimulate our creativity to run its course. We can prepare our creations and our emotional selves for going public. Do you have any such incomplete creative works that may be keeping you from moving forward? Can you find a way to finish them? Who can you share them with?

Our feminine ties to Mother Nature can be helpful here. For example, the mother bird provides a model for our need to detach from our creative products. She patiently keeps her eggs warm until the chicks are strong enough to break through their shells. Then she feeds and teaches them until they have the strength and skills to fly on their own. The chicks, if they had the choice, would probably stay in their comfortable nest forever. But at the right time, the mother bird knows when to kick them out. The young birds are on their own.

Likewise, we must trust our feminine nature to tell us when the right time has come to kick our creative works out of the nest. Testing our creative efforts in the marketplace gives us the opportunity to learn from reviews and audience reaction. Then we can decide which criticisms are worthwhile. A vital element in our assuming a place in society equal to men's is the public display of our art, publication of our books, corporate support for our projects, and recognition of the various ways we express our creativity. And we find within our unique process the courage to go public with works embodying our deep feelings.

Be Prepared for Provoking a Response

Gazing into the Grand Canyon challenges the human mind to comprehend an almost unfathomable beauty. In places a narrow strip of the Colorado River can be seen over four thousand feet below. Layers of multicolored, multitextured earth exposed by the river reveal millions of years of Earth's evolution. Our inner self, like the Grand Canyon, is composed of many fascinating layers.

When women create, we're reaching into these internal levels. A new variation on a recipe or a quick solution to a problem emerges from our lighter layers. The painting or book with universal themes reaching across cultures and generations arises from the deepest levels of our psyche. But they are all creative endeavors. In calling an act creative, the depth is irrelevant. Too often we dismiss our lighter levels of creativity, believing that only the deeper layers are creative. The first time we do something new, we've acted creatively. Affirming that act is important—because others may not; they may even be upset by our creative works.

Ingression

Our inward creative journey usually begins when some idea, feeling, or image strikes us with enough force to gain our attention. It piques our curiosity: "I wonder what would happen if I put this together with this and this?" We're hooked. So we combine that motivating force with a lifetime of experience, knowledge, and emotional growth, and we travel inward. Our path spirals through our inner layers until we connect a feeling with our original idea, feeling, or image. This combination is then brought forth on our spiral path.

At this point we take a look at our product, whether it is tangible or intangible. If we don't like what we see, we go inward once more, taking along all our skills and abilities as we did the first time. The creative union takes place again and we come up with a new product. This process continues until we are satisfied. As we express the product in completed form, we detach from it. ◄

See
Keep It Private—For a While
p. 49

The process of taking our knowledge, experience, and skill along on this inner journey and combining them with a feeling is what I call *ingression*. This phenomenon is unique to women's creative process and gives rise to a powerful product. But because of the emotional content, that product can also be intimidating or even frightening to some people. For example, if I deny my anger, pretend I'm not angry when I am, or if I'm afraid to feel my anger, I will be uncomfortable with anything that makes me aware of that anger. So I'm not going to want to look at or even be near a painting or anything else that reminds me of anger.

In the early pre-patriarchal mythology, Persephone as Queen of the Underworld demonstrates that ingression is part of our feminine nature. Her inner instincts tell her when to begin the inward journey. She travels with confidence and self-assurance, knowing what she's doing is right for her. This phenomenon is very different from the experience of being forced into the depths and becoming depressed. When Persephone completes her task of initiating the dead into their new world, she leaves the underworld, returning to her ordinary life a changed woman. This myth describes our journey inward as natural and welcomed, as are changes resulting from the process. The more we develop our relationship with our creativity, increasing our trust in the process, the more we learn to rely on ingression.

Provoking a Response

As we increase our comfort with this process, we find deeper levels of our inner selves opening to us. From our depths arise universal feelings and symbolism we can incorporate into creative works. This is true whether we are solving a business problem or writing science fiction. The feelings and universality in our endeavors bring a power to our products that are not found in lighter works, and they can evoke a strong, sometimes negative, response from others. The experience of a client demonstrates this phenomenon.

Betty is an artist who creates from deep levels of her inner self. Her work typically originates in the feminine, depicting her deep feelings through universal symbols. She has worked many years developing her talent and her relationship with her creativity to arrive at this point in her art. Yet she was still very upset by an incident for which she was unprepared.

" *I* was very excited and flattered when Sharon, the owner of several prestigious art galleries, saw some of my work in a recent show and asked me to bring three pieces to her gallery for possible exhibition. But when I showed her my paintings, Sharon gasped and stepped backward. She tried discussing the art with me, but seemed very uncomfortable. After a few minutes, she suggested moving to a different room in the gallery to continue talking. It seemed like she couldn't be in the same room with my paintings.

Finally, she urged me to take my work to a nearby, equally prestigious gallery. Sharon told me that since she only carried men's work, handling a female artist would be inappropriate.

"I've been upset by what happened for several weeks. It's not the rejection—the other gallery accepted my work. I'm really bothered by Sharon's initial reaction to my paintings. And on top of that, I can't understand why I am so bothered, so disturbed by the entire event. **"**

In discussing the incident, I learned the gallery owner was a rigid woman who conducted her business in a very aggressive manner. She related well to men and their work but avoided women. She gave the appearance of being male-defined rather than self-defined. This type of woman is usually so much in the habit of covering up her feeling responses that she has minimal awareness of those feelings. The intense symbolism in the artist's work apparently touched the owner deeply, making her very uncomfortable. The degree of discomfort she exhibited with the paintings showed the level of disquiet she experienced with her feelings.

My client's task was coping with this type of response. Detachment is the key. Once she realized how deeply her art could touch an individual, she was able to let go of her concern about the response.

When women create from our inner selves, we can expect to provoke an occasional strong response. We can also anticipate that the individual caught up in the emotional reaction may deny what's happening. For instance, the gallery owner obviously knew she was looking at quality artwork, since she recommended another gallery to the artist. Then she extracted herself diplomatically from what became an uncomfortable situation. We can't expect her or anyone else in a similar circumstance to openly state she won't handle the work because it evokes deep emotions with which she cannot deal. The individual caught in such a reaction may not even be aware of why she or he feels uncomfortable.

A friend once shared her experience with the power of our creative endeavors to provoke a response. This woman, who paints as a hobby, was working with a psychiatrist on growth-related issues. One day, my friend decided for no particular reason to take several recently completed paintings to her therapy session.

One painting is egg-shaped, with colorful designs inside. It reminds me of the Chinese yin-yang symbol. The artist calls it "Androgyne." Another contains bold circular strokes which seem to encase an indefinable yet soft mass. I related the painting to an embryo and the start of new life. This was apparently the artist's vision as well, since she named it "The Embryo." The third painting, entitled "Tree of Life," consists of a central form with many circular lines emanating from it. Unlike her usual methodical approach, these works were done quickly. To the artist, they were fun.

The psychiatrist, however, had a different reaction. She drew back from the paintings in apparent repulsion, informing my friend that she needed immediate hospitalization. The therapist was ready to commit her client to a mental institution on the basis of her reaction to the paintings.

For a different type of person this experience could have been devastating to many aspects of the personality, especially to creativity. People are sometimes institutionalized because their behavior frightens someone. Ironically, while the patient examines her actions, the frightened individual can go back to feeling safe without looking at her own behavior. If creativity is involved, the targeted person may make the unhealthy decision to repress any further relationship with her creative processes.

My friend dealt with the psychiatrist's reaction by gathering her paintings, leaving the office, and finding a new, more stable therapist. Two weeks later she received an apology from the psychiatrist, who acknowledged her overreaction and admitted that the paintings had, indeed, touched several deep, unresolved emotional issues.

As a side note, this story shouldn't frighten anyone away from seeing a therapist. The objective, supportive guidance that therapy can provide is important to personal growth. But finding a professional who understands the nature of women's creative process and who is comfortable with it is crucial.

Coping with Strong Responses

We can deal with strong, feeling responses to our work by emotionally detaching from it, as discussed in the previous section. Allowing our creative process to take its natural course enables this healthy separation to happen. Then we won't be as likely to take the reaction personally. Understanding the dynamics of what can occur will also help us cope in a positive manner. We can decide how much we want to openly communicate. Challenging or confronting the other person about the response may drive that individual into a more negative state. Or the confrontation may help us feel more confident about our work. It may also be appropriate to simply acknowledge the person's reaction, suspending judgments. One artist once told me, "I don't care how people react to my work—just so they have *some* reaction!"

The power of our creativity to touch people deeply deserves respect. When we allow others their unique reactions to our work, we are honoring their ability to be in touch with feelings that are usually inaccessible to them or uncomfortable for them.

While our society is geared toward comfort, in truth we often move forward in our maturation from a place of discomfort. Although most people don't like it, uneasiness can be a very healthy sensation. For example, if a behavior no longer works for us in its usual, familiar way and becomes disturbing instead, then we'll begin the process of changing that behavior. Our creative works can bring about the kind of disturbance from which people evolve into healthier, more mature adults. Or people can be frightened by their reactions, directing their fear in the form of negative criticism at the creator.

As we continue to develop our creativity, reaching into ever-deeper layers of our selves, we need to be aware that those profound levels will be embodied in our creative works. These may provoke a response in others who view, read, or hear our products. Our understanding of these reactions keeps us detached from them and prevents negative responses from stifling our continued creative growth.

$\mathcal{L}$earning to Accept Nurturance

The Nurturer

For at least five thousand years women have been enculturated to be caregivers. We're supposed to nurture everyone around us. Within the home and family, we are in charge of everything from our husband's and children's physical and emotional well-being to cleaning to meals to caring for the yard and garden. Thousands of years of practice have gone into orchestrating these complexities, providing us with many opportunities for exercising our holistic processes. But this heavy emphasis on being the nurturer has also created some significant problems.

The accompanying message most of us learned was, "Don't accept any nurturing for yourself." In other words, give but don't receive. But as long as we're following this negative advice, we're failing to renew ourselves. At the most basic level, supporting others without nurturing ourselves depletes energy necessary for developing creativity. For instance, the activities in this book take time and energy. If we're taking care of everyone else, we probably won't put out the energy and effort to develop our creative selves. But know this: the more we express ourselves creatively, the more we encourage creativity in others. Let's take a closer look at how this dynamic affects our creativity.

Too many women have difficulty accepting others' support, suffering physical and emotional distress after years of living such an unbalanced life. We resist changing this pattern because we believe receiving nurturance is selfish. And selfish is bad. Somehow it's OK for everyone else to take our nurturing, but it's not OK for us to accept someone else's support.

What happens as a result? Obsessed with doing everything to our highest level of competence, we become Super Manager, Super Teacher, and Super Mom, pouring emotional support out to anyone who needs it. And our intellectual, emotional, and creative energies are drained in the process. Privately, we may be heard to complain that we never get the kind of support we want from our boss, employees, husband, or children. We may become bitter and angry, or turn into a whining martyr. We exhaust our energy being enthusiastic about everyone else's creative efforts and have no energy left to support our own. All the while, we reject support from others because we don't want to be selfish.

As long as we continue taking care of everyone except ourselves, we can't nurture the development of our creativity. Most of us enjoy giving support to others and feel good when they accept our assistance. We usually feel rejected when our help is declined. Yet, ironically, when we refuse the assistance of others, we're not allowing them the satisfaction of giving to us. *That's* selfish! Besides, if we're so good at nurturing others, why can't we be just as good at nurturing ourselves?

Healthy Selfishness

To begin bringing balance into our lives, we need to exercise what I call *healthy selfishness*. This practice starts with recognizing that only by taking care of ourselves can we have anything to offer anyone else. We will surely fail to encourage creativity in our employees, students, or children without being creative ourselves.

Moving toward healthy selfishness is a big step for many women, but a necessary one for living a balanced life. At the foundation of an attitude of positive selfishness lies the notion that we're each responsible for the pleasure we derive from what we do. I'm not suggesting we ought to be striving toward 100 percent enjoyment from everything. That's unrealistic. What I am proposing is an examination of our motives for taking on a particular responsibility. Am I prompted by a grudging sense of obligation to my employer or my family? Or is it that "I gave my word, so I have to do this"? Too often accompanying such motivations is the feeling, "I don't really want to do this, but I'm obligated to," as if some outside force made the decision for us and compelled us to act.

We don't do anything we don't want to do. If we really had no desire to do something, we wouldn't. I often find resistance to this notion, but once accepted, it can radically change our motivations. When I decide I'm choosing to do something because I want to, my decision comes from within. I still may not like what I'm doing, but when I realize I choose to do it, I'm in charge. My motivation for action comes from a place of doing something for me and perhaps for someone else. I may be doing a favor for another person, but if I'm motivated by feeling good for having done it, I'm practicing healthy selfishness. I gain a sense of satisfaction from accomplishing something beneficial for someone else. With this kind of motivation, we avoid the exhausting feeling of doing everything for others. We achieve things for ourselves and prevent ourselves from becoming drained. Healthy selfishness is compatible with being supportive of others. A phrase I learned from the Kuroda Institute, a Zen center in Los Angeles, summarizes healthy selfishness: "To benefit oneself and to benefit others are like two wings of a bird."

Using this perspective, we can learn to be attuned to unhealthy situations that deplete our energy. For example, it's unhealthy for us to continually provide support and encouragement for another person's creative efforts when that individual fails to give us the same nurturance in return. We wouldn't knowingly consume spoiled food, so why would we knowingly participate in any relationship which damages our journey toward living creatively?

Mothering or Delegating?

Giving without taking has more negative implications when we carry it into the workplace. As women moved into careers outside the home, we assumed the same stance we had always taken in the home—we're in charge of everything and must do all the work ourselves. In other words, we still act as if we're the principal nurturers. This attitude often shows itself through difficulty delegating tasks—a common criticism of women in management. We frequently justify our reluctance to share projects with others by stating, "I know I can do a better job, so it's easier for me to just do it myself. If I give it to someone else, chances are I'll have to fix what they've done so it will be done right." This attitude locks us into an unhealthy role and detracts from our creative resources.

When we take on a task rather than assigning it to someone else, we may be trying to rescue that individual from making mistakes with the project. While the excuse may be that we "want it done right," what we are really doing is taking care of that other person. We're trying to keep that employee from being embarrassed by producing inferior work or from being frustrated by a difficult task or from having to confront a demanding higher-up. Or we may not want to see how someone else would do the task. These reasons may not be in our conscious awareness, but they often underlie much of our inability to delegate.

This situation results in problems for everyone involved. The other person is deprived of the learning that happens from creating something new and/or from making mistakes. She or he is also cheated out of the opportunity to grow professionally and personally. The manager or teacher who keeps her employees or students in this situation is failing to offer guidance and experience that will help them develop, and she's also keeping them dependent on her. Meanwhile, she's allowing herself to be overworked, neither asking for nor accepting help from others. She doesn't have the energy or the time to develop her creativity. All of this can happen under the guise of "I want it done right."

We've needed to learn to delegate for a long time. And many women have tackled the problem and made progress toward resolving it. We readily offer our abilities and knowledge to those around us, encouraging them to take risks and explore their own potential. We give generously of ourselves so others benefit. But too often we've done this while refusing to accept their support. In either of these scenarios, we've caused ourselves the same problem: When you support others and fail to accept nurturance from them, you aren't taking care of you.

The Balance

The place to start developing a balance between giving and accepting nurturance is within ourselves. We have to believe in healthy selfishness and accept the nurturance we rightfully deserve. Accepting this belief as a rational concept is one level, but we must also take it in at our deepest feeling level. Remember: Only by renewing ourselves can we continue in our personal evolution. Growing takes energy!

I realize that what I'm asking here is for you to overcome thousands of generations of programming. This is a radical step—one that many of you have already taken. I congratulate you and encourage your progress. For most of us, this effort is ongoing, requiring steady vigilance. Monitoring any sabotaging messages takes constant attention. Watch out for the small ways you may have of rejecting nurturance; these add up quickly. And they're often easily overlooked.

For example, too many of us still cannot accept a gift from ourselves. This issue was demonstrated by a client who has built her career in a "helping profession," working at the management level for almost twenty years. She explained:

> It's important to me to do the best job I can, at work and at home. My husband's work is stressful, so I want to be there for him. And right now my children need me. I'm proud of my management skills. I've learned to be fair and supportive of my employees, but I can be tough when I need to. I'm confident that my boss knows he can depend on me. So I just don't have much time for myself. Besides, when I try to do something just for me, I feel guilty. I even feel guilt twinges when I call you to make a therapy appointment!

I generally view guilt as unproductive, serving to keep us stuck in our own regrets. But in this case I suggested to my client that she allow her guilt to be a signal that she is about to do something good for herself. In other words, as soon as she starts feeling guilty, she knows she is close to doing something nurturing. Her next step is letting go of the guilt and taking care of her needs.

If we can't embrace something from ourselves, we can't genuinely welcome it from someone else. "Oh, you shouldn't have," said in response to a gift, can indicate reluctance to accept both the item offered and the emotional support that may come with it. Try some of these suggestions:

Practice giving yourself gifts frequently. You might buy yourself flowers, enroll in an interesting class, or take quiet time for a hike or reading. How about a peaceful bubble bath? Or a drive in the country with no particular destination? Treat yourself to some clothing accessory— scarf, belt, pin, something fun or outrageous. Then wear it! Do an activity you consider decadent, like going to a movie in the middle of a weekday afternoon or eating tacos for breakfast. You might devote yourself to some of the activities in this book. Whatever you choose, affirm as you accept your gift that you are worthy of receiving it.

For some women the difficulty with this issue shows itself in another simple way—accepting a compliment. A sincere compliment is intended to be relished as a bit of nurturance. Taking in someone else's positive feedback ought to be accompanied by a sense of confirmation. The outer statement connects with the inner belief. In other words, "You did a great job" can be absorbed to support the same inner feeling. This is the ideal.

But instead, many women immediately reject the compliment, dismissing either externally or internally what the other person has said. Instead of accepting it, the compliment, "You did a great job," might be pushed away with something like, "But I still have so much to do," spoken out loud or silently. Or it can be negated by an inner, conflicting belief such as, "I didn't do it the way you wanted me to, so it's not so great." Every time we reject a compliment, we refuse to take in something positive about ourselves. It's as if we continually push away nutritious food and then wonder why we're starving. We've resisted someone's small offer of support. To begin learning healthier behavior, we can give ourselves compliments and accept them into our inner self. The following activity can get you started in the right direction.

Start the day by looking at yourself in the mirror and giving and accepting some positive statement—spoken out loud—about yourself: "I like your hair." "You look great today." "You're a considerate person. And I like that." Whether you focus on your outward appearance or your inner self is unimportant. Monitor your internal reaction to your compliments, striving for comfortable acceptance of them. Repeat each statement many times out loud until you feel yourself absorbing it at your deepest levels.

Every morning Margaret Mead bellowed in her largest, most affirming voice, "Thank God I'm Margaret Mead!"[1] This is perhaps the ultimate compliment we can give ourselves—to be grateful we are who we are. Try your own version of this proclamation first thing in the morning, belting it out with conviction. If your first effort is weak, high-pitched, thin, and unconvincing, try again. Taking a deep breath, proclaim your gratitude in a deep, resonant voice, starting from your toes and filling your entire body. This can improve your whole day. If other members of your household are disturbed by your behavior, encourage them to join you.

When co-workers and friends offer support, learn to say yes. You may have to pause to prevent an automatic "No thanks; I can handle it myself" from escaping your lips as you wrestle with reservations about allowing this person to assist you. Remind yourself that accepting support from others is as nurturing to them as it is to you. Each time you say yes, you'll move closer to maintaining a healthier balance of giving and receiving. From this balance comes the energy you need for developing your creativity.

Quieting the Inner You

The Receiver

People sometimes think creativity functions like a television set. The signal starts at the transmission tower, travels the airwaves, and is picked up by your set. If the picture goes haywire, the problem is usually found at the signal's origin or at some point between there and the television antenna. In making this analogy, we assume if ideas aren't readily accessible, something must be wrong with the source of the creativity. In reality the reverse is true. The difficulty is with the receiver, not with the transmitter. Creative concepts are always available, but we have to learn how to listen to them. And women have some natural processes that ought to make being receptive to our unique ideas easy.

When women create, we gather all our experiences, knowledge, and wisdom, and we travel within ourselves. ◀ We've also found goddesses who demonstrate that going within is a natural part of the feminine, tied to our creative aspect. So if we're gifted with all this ability for inner reflection to enhance our creative process, why is it so hard to keep our mental receiver properly tuned to readily accept transmissions from our creative self?

See
Be Prepared for Provoking a Response
p. 57

Static

Several difficulties can inhibit the reception of our best creative efforts. First, our minds seem to always be occupied with some thought

Challenges

or thoughts which express themselves as a continuous flow of inner monologue—chatter. As long as this stream of verbiage is kept in motion, we can't hear the message our creative self is sending. Our challenge is to still the internal chatter so we can be receptive to inspirations.

Second, creativity is often a solitary process, encouraged when it's free from outside distractions. We have to allow time for ourselves so our creative process, like any living thing, can grow and mature. But some of us are uncomfortable being alone. Or we allow our lives to constantly involve others, so finding solitary time is difficult. At issue here is whether we're willing to give ourselves the solitude we need to encourage our creativity.

Next, being creative almost always involves taking chances, which is usually unsettling. To overcome the fear of risk-taking, we must trust our process to be there for us. The more we rely on our creativity, the more we open ourselves to our creative potential. As this cycle continues, trust in the process increases, thereby reducing any apprehensions around risk-taking. We know what to expect. Our creativity responds to this confidence by being even more accessible when we need it to be. A writer once described this state to me when she said, "I do think that you hold all kinds of possible thoughts and magical things inside of you, and if you trust them enough, maybe you let them out at the right time." Highly creative women trust their creativity. Trust in the process can offset misgivings about taking risks. ▶

Finally, tying our feelings to our creative products can inhibit reception of creative ideas. As an integral part of our creative process, we connect a feeling with a thought or another feeling. ◀ If we're uncomfortable with our emotions and reluctant to allow ourselves to be in contact with them, our creative process will be inhibited. Our creative efforts will be kept on a superficial level where we have access to feel-

Trust

See
Is It Quicksand or a Rock?
p. 203

See
Keep It Private—For a While
p. 49

ings we're accustomed to expressing. Until we become comfortable with inner feelings, our creative efforts will lack the power that comes from accessing our depths.

Clearing the Chatter

These challenges can provide a framework for improving communication with our creative self—by quieting internal chatter, finding comfort in being alone, trusting the process, and feeling at ease with our emotions. While these issues can be dealt with simultaneously, proceeding in small steps is advisable. I'm not encouraging anyone to climb to the highest diving platform and plunge headfirst into a black-bottomed pool of unknown depth. Sometimes we think we need to do everything immediately, if not sooner. When we're talking about developing the creative self so our creativity becomes an integral part of our daily lives, we need to take a step at a time, growing in solid ways rather than in great leaps which may prove to have no support.

Each time you acknowledge your creative efforts, you take a step. When you incorporate an activity from this book into your daily routine, you take a step. Dealing with each of the challenges described here moves you forward as well. What step(s) did you take yesterday or today to move you closer to your creative self?

By quieting internal interferences we can develop an inner ear for listening to and trusting our creative voice. Accomplishing this takes commitment and discipline, but the rewards in increased creativity are worth the effort. An excellent way to learn how to communicate with ourselves is through meditation. In a meditative state internal chatter is stilled while inner channels of communication are opened. We become familiar with our inner selves and increasingly comfortable with our unique processes. While flashes of creative insight may not happen during the meditation, at other times, when creative inspiration is needed, we'll be attuned to receive it.

Because we have so many distractions, setting aside the same time each day for meditation is important. The most benefit is derived from meditating during our highest-energy times during the day, not the lowest. In other words, a morning person will probably fall asleep meditating during the afternoon. This activity will be more powerful if the same physical place, designated only for meditation, is used consistently. Some people set aside the corner of a bedroom or their office strictly for meditation. Sometimes the same effect can be gained from sitting in a chair that has been turned in a direction it does not normally face. The idea is to set aside a space reserved for meditation.

While some advocates of meditation insist that certain rules be followed—we must face East, we must meditate an hour every day—I find that most people are put off by these demands. For purposes of encouraging inner communication between the conscious self and the creative self, our meditative efforts need to be directed to that end. As little as fifteen minutes a day can greatly contribute to our progress.

Most people have difficulty shutting off their internal chatter when they begin to meditate. An effective way to deal with this is to give that chattering part something to do. We can accomplish this through an ancient breathing technique which is easy to master:

Begin by sitting comfortably in a chair or on a pillow. (Most people fall asleep if they lie down to meditate.) Focus on your breathing. Follow your breath in with your awareness, then follow it back out. Paying close attention to your breathing quiets the brain by giving it something on which to focus. Do this for a few minutes, until you feel yourself beginning to relax. Now slowly and evenly inhale to the count of seven. Hold the breath for one count, then exhale to the count of seven. Hold the exhale for one count. Continue in that pattern, 7-1-7-1, for as long as you like, giving yourself at least ten minutes with it. This ancient meditation quickly focuses your attention on your inner self. The counting quiets any internal noise.

If you're like most people, the first few times you try inhaling to the count of seven you may find that you have filled your lungs by the time you reach four. When you exhale, you've emptied your lungs by the count of three. Some people resist holding the exhale, wanting instead to inhale quickly to catch a breath. These difficulties usually last only a brief time before the breathing is evenly following the prescribed rhythm.

This technique is excellent to use during stressful times of the day. You can slip into the 7-1-7-1 breathing pattern while sitting at your desk or in a meeting or behind the wheel of your car. It will have a calming effect on your entire body, including your brain, so you can think and create more clearly and rid yourself of some of the negative effects of stress.

In "Understanding Your Feminine Nature" ◀ the activity designed to develop the feminine aspect through close communion with Nature is a type of meditation. When we're at one with Nature, inner channels are opening to our creative self. We can combine our efforts to nurture the feminine with learning how to meditate.

Many books describing various meditation techniques have been written. For our purposes in developing creativity, the intent is to control internal interferences which prevent us from hearing our creative self. Through meditation we can develop a finely adjusted inner ear attuned to listening to our creative self.

See
**Understanding
Your Feminine
Nature**
p. 39

*D*eveloping a
Sense of Timing

Nature always knows when the right time has come for certain events to happen—for the baby bird to leave its nest, for the snake to shed its skin, for the bear to hibernate. And this instinctive sense of timing resides within the feminine. It's one of the most helpful gifts our feminine self brings to us. In developing creativity, we need to nurture a sense of timing about our creative works, to develop an inner knowing about when to be active and when to be passive.

This awareness can be applied throughout our daily lives, especially during interactions with others. Knowing exactly when to bring up a delicate issue in a personal relationship can make the difference between a positive outcome and a negative one. And no one can be in the business world very long without hearing the phrase, "Timing is everything." Common sense tells us to avoid making a new proposal to someone who is clearly overwhelmed by immediate demands. We want an attentive audience for our creative works. Yet intuitively knowing when the right time has come to present a creative idea to the boss or when to talk over a difficult situation with an employee probably can't be learned. This instinct, arising from the feminine, knows when to bring up an issue for discussion and when to remain quiet. It knows how to present information so our target audience will listen.

A finely tuned sense of timing is valuable in the business world, in the classroom, or in dealing individually with people. We can use it when we are coping with a touchy family problem or deciding who to hire or motivating students to learn. Like other aspects of our creativity and our feminine, the more we follow this intuitive timing, the more it will be present when needed. Making use of the messages our feminine sends us encourages both our trust in this process and our awareness of it. And trusting that our sense of timing will be there for us is the first step in developing this function.

This instinctive sense of timing is often communicated through the body, through a "gut" feeling of what is right or wrong. Establishing a clear connection with the body is important as we develop our sense of timing. The following activity is designed to teach attunement to this inner sensation.

Give yourself at least thirty minutes for this activity. Begin by sitting comfortably in a place where you won't be disturbed. Close your eyes and pay attention to your breathing. Follow your breath in with your awareness, then follow it back out. Do this for at least ten breaths or until you begin feeling relaxed.

Now direct your attention to different parts of your body, one part at a time, allowing about thirty seconds for each. Pay attention to your hands, then to your shoulders, to your feet, to your abdomen, to your brain. Have fun with this, skipping your attention from one area of your body to another. Or move sequentially, bottom to top or top to bottom.

Now focus on smaller parts, such as your right thumb, your left little toe, the end of your nose. Keep your attention on each one long enough to gain a full sensation of it.

Now attend to your breathing once again and sense your whole body at once, all the individual parts now united.

At this point, begin an inner dialogue with your feminine self. Ask that part of you to come into your awareness, to be present and clear so you can communicate with each other. Once you've established this connection, tell it your intent—to become attuned to your inherent sense of timing so you can rely on it. You may have to state your purpose several times. When you feel that your feminine self has heard your intention, ask it for help.

Ask your feminine aspect to let you feel the sensation in your body that will tell you when something is right—when the timing is appropriate to present a creative idea, for example, or whatever application you have in mind. Allow the sensation to be presented to you. Be open to what you feel and where you might feel it. You may need to ask again, clearly stating your intent. Remember the feeling you sense in response and know that when you experience this sensation, you're on the right track.

Now ask your feminine to present you with the sensation in your body that will tell you when to avoid taking some action. Ask your feminine to give you the feeling you can associate with the need to be passive. Just as before, remember this sensation and know that when you have this feeling, your feminine is telling you to wait.

Finally, thank your feminine for giving you this information. Assure it you will honor it by paying attention to the signals as they are given.

Sometimes the sensation your feminine gives is too "loud" to be effective. For instance, you probably don't need a stomachache just to know when to be still about an idea. If your feminine self presents you with a bodily sensation that is too drastic to be useful, you can negotiate for a more effective feeling. Instead of a stomach cramp, you can ask your feminine to give you a slight twinge.

If you're an especially strong visual person, your feminine may give you a mental picture, such as the words *yes* or *no* or an image of what to do, depending on the purpose. A strong auditory individual may hear these words inside her head. Your feminine will present the message to you in the right way so you can most effectively receive it.

You may need to take yourself through this activity several times in order to gain a clear sensation. You're asking yourself to communicate with yourself in a new way. This usually takes some time and patience. Once you've gained a clear sensation of how these active/passive messages are communicated through your body, take notice of them during the day. When they present themselves to you, honor them. And thank your feminine for sending the message. If you're in a situation where you need some clear direction and you're not receiving it, ask for it. You'll have one more tool from within yourself that you can use to enhance your creativity and make the most effective presentation of your creative works.

$\mathscr{A}$ Room of Your Own

Sacred space and sacred time form two essential ingredients in developing creativity. Cultivating creative talents and giving form to creative endeavors requires uninterrupted time enjoyed in a special place. *Sacred space* is our own room, our office, our niche. When we're in it, no one enters who isn't invited. *Sacred time* is the part of the day devoted to creative work. We may use sacred time for doing some of the activities described in this book or for working on creative projects. No one else will provide these things for us; we need to create them for ourselves.

While the home has traditionally been women's domain, we've had to share it with everyone. And we've extended this experience into the work setting, so we often get ourselves into situations of being frequently interrupted. These intrusions can happen even if we're fortunate enough to have our own office at work or our own room at home. The challenge is to make others respect our sacred space and time.

But we often find ourselves in the dilemma of feeling selfish when we think about insisting on doing something for ourselves. In our efforts to develop a relationship with our creativity, we can exercise our prerogative of healthy selfishness to establish sacred space and time. ◀ We're in charge of giving ourselves what we need to develop our creativity. Any woman trying to engage in creative work must demand the physical space and the quiet time to nurture a relationship with her creativity. The situation one author described to me illustrates this need:

See
Learning to Accept Nurturance
p. 65

" *I* started writing books when my children were in elementary school. Working while they were in school was easy. And I got the necessary housework done during the half hour just before they got home. But I still had to balance writing and children during weekends and summer vacations. Even though I told my children not to bother me when I was in my room writing, they were reluctant to leave me alone. Typically, they would intrude, badgering me with questions and complaints. And they encountered a very cranky mother. So they quickly learned if they left me alone, allowing me to write undisturbed, they would later enjoy an attentive mother in a good mood. I had my sacred space and sacred time! "

Carving Out Your Domain

The first step in setting up sacred space is believing that we deserve it. If we want to make art, we need a room devoted to that endeavor. If we want to write, we need a place where our notes and papers will be undisturbed. If we want to come up with an innovative way to solve a company problem, we need a place where we can thoroughly research the project.

In order to establish sacred space at home, we'll need to enlist the aid of others in the household. We may want to involve them in deciding which room will be ours. If an entire room is available, great. If not, space can be fashioned by separating part of a room with a screen. One client who reached the decision to pursue an art career was fortunate to have a supportive husband. At his suggestion, they enclosed part of a porch in the rear of their house for her studio.

Regardless of the physical setup, others in the household must learn that our space is to be undisturbed. Clear rules must be established at the outset: when we're working, no interruptions. Violations of this agreement have to be dealt with firmly. Family members can suddenly come up with urgent questions or needs designed to get our attention. If we've involved everyone at the outset, gaining their support for our creative efforts, they can be reminded of their commitment. Then we can get back to our project.

For Julie, an artist and musician, sacred space is so important she allows no one into her studio. She explains, "There is a point in the course of writing a song or painting a painting where, for any other human being to come into the space where it is being created, it would interrupt, destroy the natural completion, and would forever change or alter what needed to unfold."

In the work world the situation may be somewhat more difficult. Having a separate office certainly provides an advantage. But many "offices" are divided by six- or eight-foot-high partitions with no door. In this situation, the tone can be set by respecting others' privacy and not intruding on them when they're working. Or if we're interrupted during our creative work, we can politely inform the other individual that we're busy, then offer to make an appointment for a later time. If our workspace consists of a desk in a large room with many other desks, we can create psychological space around the desk, constructing an office without walls. Creating our own space at home becomes even more important when we don't have privacy at work. Not surprisingly, many women tell me they have learned to cope with lack of privacy by creating sacred space anywhere they need it. A journalism professor stated, "I can create a space wherever I am. I 'will' a quiet zone around myself, blocking out noise and distractions." Likewise, when asked about sacred space, a therapist simply said, "I carry it with me!"

Taking Your Time

Establishing sacred time also requires a commitment to developing creativity. With this motivation, a certain amount of time is set aside each day for working with our creativity. We might be meditating or enjoying nature or working on a particular project. We may choose time at home or at work. What's important is devoting this time to meeting creative needs and encouraging or demanding that people around us respect it as ours alone.

Women who work at home, whether painting, writing, or running a small business, face unique challenges with sacred time. Because we're home most of the time, friends and family can easily perceive us as not really working. They think nothing of calling to chat on the telephone in a way they wouldn't call someone working outside the home. Or they drop by for a surprise visit. Women whose workplace is the home often have to train friends and family to respect this work situation. A creative thought interrupted by the telephone or a knock on the door may be gone forever. Answering machines are a necessity for these women, as is resisting the temptation to answer the door. Our creative work is too important to be disturbed. Eventually, friends and family members learn that by respecting our sacred space and time, they're supporting our creative efforts.

Inevitably, women who say they simply cannot have quiet time at work are allowing others to control their time. "I am constantly interrupted" is the excuse of the inefficient. Granted, gaining sacred time is usually more difficult for, say, a secretary than it is for a manager. The latter can request that her secretary handle all calls and notify everyone that she is in a "meeting." But secretaries can make opportunities for sacred time, too. Rotating phone-answering responsibilities with peers may be one idea. Color-coded signs have also been effective in gaining privacy in some settings. For example, putting a green placard on your desk can mean interruptions are OK, while a red one means stay away.

For the office consisting of partitions, a PLEASE DO NOT DISTURB sign can be posted near the "door." I know one woman with this style office who wears ear protectors to mute loud noises. It's her signal that she needs her quiet time for working on a project. Her co-workers have learned not to disturb her when they see her wearing the all-too-obvious ear covers.

In some work situations, the physical space is so public we can't establish either sacred space or sacred time. In this case, having our own place and time outside of work becomes very important.

We need privacy and solitude to facilitate our creative process. Through our commitment to ourselves we'll make certain we have what we need.

$\mathcal{P}$erfectionism: Creativity's Saboteur

Symptoms

"I'm a perfectionist." The statement was intended to be an explanation. Her tone of voice bragged but her shrugged shoulders apologized. As her manager, I was supposed to accept her perfectionism as justifying an obsession with endlessly refining her work, already long overdue. Her behavior caused stress for co-workers who depended on her part of the project. And her own tension peaked at times like these as she struggled to use just the right word, the flawless phrase, to reach perfection—a state irrelevant to the task at hand.

In striving for perfection, this woman accomplished what many perfectionists achieve: increased stress, decreased productivity, irritated co-workers. No one sought her out for creative input into any project. She was plagued by several stress-related physical disorders. Still, she felt pride in being a perfectionist, oblivious to the costs.

Creativity and perfection, like oil and water, don't mix. Expressing ourselves creatively requires us to assume risks, make mistakes, experiment with the unknown, and take leaps of faith. These activities occur only when we're energized by a spirit of adventure and curiosity.

The creative woman who is also devoted to perfectionism sabotages her creativity in many ways. She wants everything to be "just right" before she'll even consider doing something different. Her fear of being less-than-perfect encourages her to procrastinate on starting anything new. When she makes a mistake, her tunnel vision is activated so she sees only the error, not her accomplishments. She's paralyzed. So is her creativity.

The perfectionist's expectations of herself are unrealistically high. Her first book must be a best-seller. Her art must be shown by the finest gallery in New York. Her boss must accept her ideas in their entirety. Any lesser accomplishment means failure. Even when she does meet her goal, she'll decide it wasn't high enough! Her all-or-nothing attitude dismisses her unique efforts and eliminates the creative possibilities that flourish with the spontaneous and unexpected.

She can also diminish her creativity by comparing herself to others. And she'll always find someone else who writes better, paints better, or presents more useful ideas. The perfectionist and her creative works inevitably come in a distant second.

The creative spirit needs to be nurtured and encouraged. Perfectionistic behavior does the opposite by viewing the development of creativity as just another challenge to conquer. Over time, the battered creative self becomes reluctant to express itself in a healthy way. And repressed creative energy compounds the stress of every perfectionist.

The Foundation

Women are caught up in several circumstances that feed perfectionism. Encultrated to believe we're in charge of everything within our realm of responsibility—historically, the home—we've taken this attitude into the workplace. We try to do it all, taking on increasing responsibility, failing to delegate or trust others to be competent. In addition, women are rarely treated as equals by male counterparts, which often brings about pressure to prove we can do everything and anything at any time. We try to overcome our imposed secondary status by becoming indispensable. Finally, we tend to define ourselves according to multiple roles—wife, career, mother (and sometimes father), caregiver, volunteer. The perfectionist believes she must excel at all of these roles and their accompanying tasks. Men usually define themselves by only one role—that associated with their career choice.[1]

The Toll

So the perfectionist is trapped between expectations set so high they're impossible to achieve and a battered self-esteem telling her she's not good enough to deserve success. With her life designed for all-or-nothing, she usually gets nothing, even when she may look as if she has everything. With her exterior self designed for approval and acceptance, she tries to prove she doesn't need help from anyone.[2] Meanwhile her true self, that unique individual enlivened through creative expression, withers from lack of nourishment. And the physical toll is enormous. Stress-related illnesses, lowered productivity, eating disorders, substance abuse, emotional emptiness, and lack of spiritual connection are all related to perfectionism.[3] And like any addict, the perfectionist denies her addiction.

While she can maintain a perfectionistic attitude toward life for a long time, eventually, as she expects more and more from herself, her coping skills break down. The physical and emotional strain of giving increasingly of herself while cutting herself off from taking in any nourishment in return becomes overwhelming.

At this point, she may begin to feel like a stranger to herself, an incompetent stranger! Troubled with forgetfulness and confusion, she may experience further declines in productivity, difficulty concentrating, and inconsistent logic.[4] Her sense of humor evaporates as her perceptions continue to dull. Pleasure becomes a remote memory. And expressing creativity is impossible. This isn't the way life is supposed to feel! But how does she break the cycle?

Recovery: Acknowledging Your Perfectionism

The first step in recovery comes when the perfectionist recognizes the damage she is inflicting upon herself and decides the price is too high. This decision is not as easy as it may sound. Being a perfectionist has undoubtedly had its rewards. This woman may have achieved a lot of external success; she may feel in control of her life. Much of her sense of accomplishment is based on being perfect. Now she has to realize that these images are illusions and be willing to give up a long-standing relationship with her perfectionist self. While this choice is clearly the healthy one, old relationships are sometimes hard to let go of.

One way to facilitate this initial step is to acknowledge what benefits have come from the perfectionism. When it is honored in its totality—pluses *and* minuses—the perfection addiction is easier to break. As is sometimes the case, this activity may be more beneficial when it is done with the aid of a therapist. Each person must use her judgment about whether to do these exercises alone. Regardless, the following activity can help with the first step toward recovery.

On a sheet of paper, make a list of all the benefits of being a perfectionist. Be as specific as you can, giving yourself adequate time to generate as many as you can think of. On a second sheet, list the downside of perfectionism, the negatives. Now on a third piece of paper, write a clear statement of your decision to give up your perfection addiction. You might write something like, "I am giving up trying to be perfect. I am choosing a healthy acceptance of who I am." However you choose to say it, just be certain your statement reflects the positive nature of your decision. Now, under this declaration, list all the benefits you expect to derive as you implement this decision in your life. Think of as many areas as you can: relationships, work, stress level, home, enjoyment of living. Create as clear an image as you can at this point of a life free from perfectionistic burdens.

Or you may want to draw a picture of what your new life looks like. This can be as literal or symbolic as you want. And use the medium that is most freeing for you: crayons, watercolors, finger or poster paints. Use both your dominant and nondominant hands when drawing.

Now, holding this image in your mind, burn the first two lists. As your perfectionism goes up in smoke, thank it for everything it has done for you and affirm that you are releasing the unhealthy aspects. Know that you are cleansing the old and energizing your new choice at the same time.

Creating Realistic Expectations

After recognizing and acknowledging her perfectionism, the recovering perfectionist must tackle behaviors and internal messages associated with striving to be perfect. A common behavior is expecting to accomplish too many tasks in one day. This dilemma can be resolved by spreading them out over several days. The perfectionist also thinks every chore must be completed as soon as possible. She needs to learn to prioritize tasks and to give herself adequate time to finish them. She may have to delegate responsibilities to others, a challenge discussed in

See
the prioritizing technique in **Procrastination and Creativity— Working Together** *p. 221*

more detail later in this chapter. In making these shifts, the recovering perfectionist may need to remind herself she wants to finish one task at a time in a reasonable amount of time with minimal stress. ▶

Goals need to be moderated so they're attainable. The perfectionist commonly rejects lowering her expectations by believing her goals won't be worth her efforts if they aren't so high she probably won't be able to reach them. This convoluted thinking can only be overcome by rejecting the all-or-nothing perspective of most perfectionists, in which one error is cause for negating all the work on a project.

A more realistic approach is striving for excellence. While perfection is impossible to achieve, excellence lies within the realm of everyone. Rather than reducing the focus to a specific goal, excellence rewards progress toward the result as well as the outcome itself. In this framework, mistakes become learning experiences. Creativity happens on the way to excellence.

So the recovering perfectionist must develop a sense of her personal best. She'll have to stop comparing herself to others—she never measures up anyway. Forgiving herself becomes important so she can learn from mistakes and then move ahead with living creatively. Unlike the perfectionist employee I cited in the beginning of this section, the woman who gives up her perfectionism takes responsibility for her actions and inactions. Since she has established her vision of excellence, she's in charge of whether or not she attains that state. She no longer has her perfectionism to keep her from changing, to provide her with the apparent comfort of procrastination. But she'll have to deal with her fears— of achieving what she set out to accomplish, of becoming a self-defined individual freed of an outer shell designed to please others, of being happy with herself.

In the work setting this recovering perfectionist will learn to accept others' standards as she delegates tasks. She'll have to trust them to complete the task to the best of their ability and give up attempting to control the outcome by imposing her standards. With rare exception, the more confidence a manager has in her employees, the more competence they will display. But to do this, she'll have to trust herself.

Nurturing, Acceptance, and Trust

Increased self-trust allows for enhanced creative expression. Risks aren't as scary when they're taken with self-confidence. A sense of personal best enables the recovering perfectionist to experience pleasure in her creative process. The need to compare herself to others stops as she trusts her internal sense of excellence. With this kind of nurturing, her creativity continues to grow, acting as an antidote to stress.

But she'll have to maintain a vigilant inner watch for the tendency to beat herself up for not being perfect. She can't expect herself to be a perfect recovering perfectionist! Self-forgiveness is the key to this process. As she moderates her expectations to a more reasonable level, she will also have to learn to be kinder to herself. Affirmations like "I enjoy being who I am" or "I accept myself in my totality" can help with this process.

Because being a perfectionist and living creatively are mutually exclusive, this book provides abundant guidelines for recovering from perfectionism. Issues needing special attention include trusting the inner self, nurturing a sense of humor, learning time and self-management skills, developing the ability to accept nurturance from self and others, and accepting responsibility for our creative efforts. Taking that critical first step toward creativity and away from perfectionism can be unsettling. The creative experience isn't a neat, tidy sequence following predictable steps. It's a free-flowing process that can seem to run in every direction at the same time, requiring nurturance, acceptance, and trust in its inherent healthiness.

If you still believe being perfect is worth striving for, think about novels you've enjoyed. Like life, books aren't made up of perfect characters. They're loaded with flawed individuals who struggle with themselves and with the outside world. People can't relate to perfection. We relate to the imperfections in others, to the qualities that make us interesting and give us the rough edges from which our creativity arises.

Understanding the Creative/Depressive Cycle

When we open ourselves to our creativity, we also open ourselves to a variety of wonderful sensations. Some of these feelings include:

- An intense aliveness and increasing confidence
- Reduced stress
- An inner sense of peace
- More control of our life
- A deep satisfaction of expressing our true self in unique and fulfilling ways.

The more we weave our creativity throughout our lives, living a creative lifestyle, the more benefits we'll experience.

Conversely, the penalties for repressing creativity are heavy. Any natural part of the human psyche needs to be expressed, and ideally, we provide a healthy outlet for this expression. But if a function is stifled, it will manifest itself negatively. The energy residing in our creative selves is extremely powerful. Failing to direct our creativity in a positive way means it will reveal itself in unhealthy behaviors. One way or the other, our creative energy will make itself felt in our lives.

Suppressing Creativity Usually Starts Early

Many studies have shown us that a young girl's ideas are frequently discounted by her peers and teachers. Being bombarded repeatedly by the message that her creative notions are no good, the young girl in this dilemma will often begin believing what others are saying. In response, she stifles her creativity. When creative ideas come, she keeps them to herself rather than taking the risk of being ignored or even ridiculed by peers and adults. She may dismiss herself, eventually squashing her creative notions and behaviors before they come to life within her. She'll be tempted to develop a false but more acceptable self which she presents to the world. This may provide her with some relief from feeling discounted, but at the same time she alienates herself from her true being, cutting off her emotions in the process. She becomes depressed, her psyche thrown into grieving for the lost self.

Repressed creativity can lead her to become very conforming, to lack confidence in her thinking, and to be overly dependent on others for decision-making. A young person caught in this circumstance runs the risk of being labeled a slow learner who is never given a challenging task stimulating to her creativity. These feelings of inadequacy naturally spill into other areas of her personality. Behavior problems commonly result, and she becomes sullen and withdrawn or agitated and troublemaking.[1]

Manifestations in Adulthood

Carried into adulthood, these maladjustments lead to a variety of behaviors. The adult who isn't expressing her creativity is falling short of her potential. Inwardly she feels this, experiencing a vague sense of dissatisfaction intruding into everything she does. I've worked with many women who have achieved high positions of authority in business yet are still plagued by these self-doubts. Such feelings often make it impossible for these women to appreciate their successes.

Worse, the extreme insecurity and dependence on others for decision-making developed in the creatively stifled child are continued into adulthood. The foundation has been formed for becoming locked into co-dependent behaviors. Until she reclaims her creative, independent self, a woman in this circumstance will be vulnerable to being involved in unhealthy relationships.

Repressed creativity can also express itself in overwhelming stress, severe neurotic or even psychotic behavior, and addictive behaviors such as alcoholism. But perhaps the most insidious and common manifestation of repressed creativity in women is depression.

Depression

Many years ago psychologist Jessie Bernard estimated that 60 percent of American women are depressed as a lifestyle.[2] These women see a dulled world, one that is more fearful than exciting, more destructive than challenging, more a place to avoid than embrace. They respond to crises with denial and withdrawal. Problems are confounding and overwhelming instead of creatively stimulating. While they certainly can live a "normal" life, they lack enthusiasm for that life. This state should not be confused with a situational depression which comes in response to a particular life event. For example, feeling depressed is a natural response to the death of a loved one, to the loss of a job, to any major change. Nor should it be confused with clinical depression, a severe, usually long-term depression which virtually immobilizes an individual and requires professional help. I certainly advise anyone dealing with any type of depression to seek the assistance of a trusted therapist. It's a joy thief that steals the life out of living.

Unfortunately, in the years since Bernard's estimate of women leading depressed lives, the numbers haven't changed. These women may have "successful" careers or they may be running households, but they lack enthusiasm for life. They often carry an inner feeling of being less than they know they could be. They judge themselves against what's been called the "goodness model," admonishing themselves to be a "good wife," "good boss," "good mother," "good employee."[3] No role escapes the judgment. And they can never measure up. Thus, these depressed women discount their accomplishments, reinforcing their low self-esteem. Their response to any crisis is to become confused, indecisive, and withdrawn. Or they overreact by becoming rigid and dogmatic. They have a lot in common with perfectionists. ◀

See
Perfectionism: Creativity's Saboteur
p. 89

In an educational system and a society that thwarts the development of creativity in almost everyone, women have had an especially difficult time gaining recognition for our creativity. It's no coincidence that as our creative works have gone unrecognized, we're suffering from depression in overwhelming numbers. In fact, depression hits twice as many women as men.[4] While a depressive disorder can have many causes, one of the most common yet overlooked is stifled creativity. Learning how to give expression to creativity can be an antidote to depression.

Many of the women I see in private practice describe a certain feeling of uneasiness about their lives. The case of Janet is typical. A career woman in her early forties, Janet also had three children and a solid marriage. She was living a life she thought would be fulfilling, but it wasn't. Janet didn't hate her life, but she knew something was missing. And she had been unable to pin down the exact reason for her inner sense of dissatisfaction.

I asked Janet to tell me about exciting things she did or inner passions she expressed. She could cite very little spontaneity or excitement or passion in any aspect of her life. Much of what she accomplished, both in her career and at home, was done for others out of a sense of obligation. Janet was typical of so many women I've seen. She had no regular outlet for her creativity and she was heavily programmed to be self-sacrificing. When she was creative, she failed to recognize it.

Janet's first challenge was learning to appreciate her creative acts, to acknowledge and honor her creativity. Once she made progress on this issue, she became afraid that if she expressed her creativity, she would make too many upsetting changes in her life. Even if it's unsatisfying, the familiar is often preferable to the unknown.

Lately, I've been hearing a stronger message from women generally ranging in age from forty-five through their fifties. They're all saying the same thing: "I'm not as happy as I thought I would be at my age. And I'm not willing to live like this any more." The last child leaving home is often the trigger for these feelings. Or sometimes it's the sense of having "maxed out" in a career. That these women have decided not to be content with being unhappy is a healthy choice. Inevitably, moving toward a happy, satisfying life means encountering, encouraging, and enhancing your creativity.

Fighting Depression with Creativity

Most women like Janet can add fulfillment to their lives by becoming more creative in their current situations. They can keep themselves out of a depression by expressing their creativity. Exploring ways to be more creative at work and in the home can add a new level of interest and challenge without completely restructuring their lives. This is the purpose of the activities in this book.

For those of you who are fearful of a change like this, please know that becoming creative doesn't necessarily mean you'll totally disrupt your lives. In my experience, only a few women have drastically restructured their lives as they learned to express their creative selves. Each of these women says she's happier in her new life than she was in the old, feeling that as she gives creative expression to her special talents, she's truly alive. So, in the end, the change was well worth the risk.

There are certain activities which are especially beneficial for pulling out of a depression and becoming more creative. When we become depressed, we turn inward, pulling in energy without putting it out. The energy *implodes*. (This explains why depressed people are so draining to be around. They literally pull energy away from us but don't give any back.) Spending some time every day developing close ties to Nature will help reverse this internalized energy. ◀ To become one with Nature, we must expand ourselves, reaching out to the tree or the bird. We can feel ourselves growing as large as all outdoors. Suddenly we're extending our energy outward, shifting the direction of the flow. The depression begins to lift.

Hiking, swimming, tennis, or any type of regular physical activity is crucial. Twenty minutes of a sustained cardiovascular workout changes brain activity and begins pulling us out of a depression. Regular exercise is important to the mental health of anyone who spends most of her time engaged in creative work. ▶

See
Understanding Your Feminine Nature
p. 39

See
Dancing with Goliath
p. 241

Do You Need to Be Depressed to Be Creative?

I know some people who make a living from their creativity who believe they can't create unless they're depressed. But in terms of how our brains function, being creative and depressed at the same time is impossible. While we're creating, our brains are very active. When we're depressed, brain activity slows down. These people may have learned to pull themselves out of a depression by exercising their creativity. While this might be a healthy activity initially, it can become unhealthy for the individual when it develops into a pattern of behavior. A dependency can be established between being depressed and being creative. The creator believes she must be depressed in order to be creative, so she won't try to avoid the depression. The individual caught in this trap rides an endless roller coaster of emotional ups and downs, which eventually takes a toll on creative expression. This cycle can be broken by learning to avoid the depression while nurturing creative expression and understanding that *depression isn't necessary in order to create*. Going within oneself and resting can be accomplished at will and should not be confused with being depressed!

Another phenomenon to be dealt with in the creative/depressive cycle involves *homeostasis*, which is the balance the brain wants to maintain between the two extremes. After an intense creative outburst, usually involving sustained creative work carried out over a period of time, the brain wants to balance itself. Once the project is completed, we may be pulled into a depression by a brain that's overcompensating. This normal part of the process can be anticipated and avoided.

Regular physical activity, engaged in throughout the creative output, keeps the brain more balanced. At the conclusion of the project, a change of scenery can also be helpful. Getting out of town for a long weekend might be enough to refresh and recharge the creative juices. Or a week or two in a foreign country may be what's called for. Whatever the remedy, the most important point is recognizing there's a natural fluctuation in brain activity. With the right kind of attention and planning, we can remain in charge of our creativity.

By understanding the creative/depressive cycle, we learn to cope with it, avoiding the depression and enjoying the creativity. We can also use our creativity to pull ourselves out of depression. Ultimately, by living a creative lifestyle, we replace the depression in our lives, fulfilling our potential and becoming who we truly are.

Where's the Passion?

Passion. The word often inspires giggles of discomfort, even among adults. They equate it with lust. But there's a lot more to passion than bedroom feelings. Everyone has at least one natural passion, something that, when we plug into it, gets our creative juices flowing. Being passionate about something means experiencing life fully, giving a voice to our innermost selves. Passion is the expression of inherent creative energy which provides a motivating force behind creative work. Our distinctive creative talents are expressed through our passions.

But if we don't give expression to our passions, or if we don't know what we're passionate about, it's difficult being enthused about anything else in life. Days drag from one routine to another, strung together by dullness. Living without passion often means we're depressed. Passion, like creativity, wants to be noticed, nurtured, and expressed. Only then does it spill into all areas of our lives, helping us become enthusiastic people living creatively.

People working to develop their creativity must inevitably encounter their inner passions, sometimes reluctantly. My clients' most common fear is discovering they're passionate about something they're not currently working at, as if they might have to disrupt their lives to pursue their "new" passions. Sometimes people do change their lives drastically as they learn more about expressing their innermost loves. But people often find they can express themselves in their current line of work, through volunteering, or with hobbies. Others learn to validate what they're already doing as an expression of their creative passion.

For example, the woman who chooses to stay at home creating a nurturing environment for the entire family has frequently been dismissed. The assumption has been that she is fulfilling a role put upon her, and if she had a choice, she would have a different career. Her efforts are grossly undervalued by society, so she may also have difficulty finding value in her work. But when she discovers she is passionate about homemaking and it allows her to express creative energies, she can learn to honor her activities. She'll soon begin demanding the same respect from others.

So we must discover what our natural passion is. We can be passionate about the debate of ideas, the formulation of solutions to problems, or the empowerment of other people. The possibilities are as varied as our interests. Once we discover and express our passion, we have our motivation for doing creative work.

When I ask women what they are passionate about, I get a variety of responses. A counselor tells me her passion lies with "honesty and justice, expressed through my work in conflict resolution." Similarly, a writer says she is passionate about justice and common sense. Another counselor states, "Passion cannot be learned—it happens when creativity is allowed to blossom and when one develops an interest in following where it leads, without attaching shoulds and the question, 'Where is the money?' to it." Women often seem to tie their passions to their work. An entrepreneur, a professional speaker, stated she is passionate "about learning to enjoy life more and to communicate that with others." She added that hummingbirds are also one of her passions.

Passion can stimulate the courage we may need to make changes or the drive necessary to stay committed to a decision. For example, developing the discipline to practice the activities in this book is a struggle for some. We are well-intended when we commit ourselves to these endeavors, but staying with our resolutions often requires more self-discipline than we're accustomed to expressing. Our motivation to stay with our new behaviors will come largely from our passions.

The process goes like this:

- As we develop our creativity, we uncover areas of natural passion. They go together. Passion is the spark that ignites the creative process, that lets us know we have enough interest in something to put our creative energy into it. Passion turns us on so that we will turn on the creative juices.
- These passions want to be expressed creatively. They need an outlet. Expressing our passions is another way of declaring, "This is me. This is who I am." As growing, changing human beings, we find a variety of unique ways to make this declaration.
- As we use our creativity to give voice to our passions, those passions increasingly want to be expressed. Like the genie who has to be released from the bottle in order to do what she's here to do—grant wishes—passions have to have an outlet. Once we find one way to express a passion, we will find other ways. Or other passions will want to be heard. Like the creative process in general, the more attention and nurturing we give to our passions, the more they will respond.
- Thus, our motivation for doing creative work arises from our passions.

While developing creativity requires effort and occasionally changes in lifestyle, expressing creative passions is a pleasurable experience. Some aspects, like practicing self-discipline, may be a grind, but overall, working with our creativity is enjoyable. Over a period of time, this pleasure becomes another motivator for doing creative work.

Understanding and expressing our passions can also give us courage to take the risks so often associated with creative action. Some people may find a few activities in this book risky, for instance. Putting our creative works out for public scrutiny means taking many risks. Innovations are often scorned. Anyone trying to earn a living as an artist or writer has been told, repeatedly, about the statistical improbability of fulfilling that dream. But being passionate about our creative endeavors enhances our resolve to overcome discouraging comments, attitudes, or experiences.

Consider the politician who stuck with his passion in spite of twenty-nine years of failures. He experienced two business bankruptcies, was defeated for the state legislature, suffered a mental breakdown, and was defeated for speaker, elector, Congress, the Senate, vice president, and the Senate again. Finally, a tenacious Abraham Lincoln was elected president. While this degree of persistence is unusual, most of us can derive some level of enthusiasm from our passion for expressing our creative needs.

Discovering our natural passions is like an internal treasure hunt. One place to begin is by recalling what you enjoyed doing around the age of eleven or twelve. Think of activities you engaged in alone or in a group, in or out of school. The interests you had during your early teen years can indicate where your natural passions lie. Look at that time in your life right before the heavy peer pressure of adolescence hit.

For example, in seventh grade I discovered the writings of Jules Verne. I read every book I could find, fascinated by the accuracy of his predictions which, in some instances, ran contrary to scientific teachings of his day. I also began writing during that time—poetry and a few maudlin juvenile short stories. I'm still intrigued with conceptualizing possible futures and I still write. I've combined these loves into a science-fiction novel. I also enjoy teaching career-exploration classes where I help others speculate about their possible futures. And I am driven to explore and develop human potential, the future of our species. This book has grown out of these interests as have my many articles and workshops devoted to human growth. My passions for writing and speculating about and constructing alternate futures are manifested in many ways.

As you think about specific activities you engaged in during your early years, look for generalizations you can make about your involvement. What did you enjoy most about the activity? What attracted you to it in the first place? What do you do now that is similar? How can you do more of it? Sometimes we've forgotten what we especially enjoyed in our early years, so asking a parent or sibling what they remember about our interests may be helpful.

Unfortunately, some of us experienced rejection as we expressed our new passions. If we suddenly developed an interest in painting but lacked the skills to make art, we may have squashed the interest rather than dealt with others' negative comments. In resurrecting that passion for art, we may choose to take painting classes, buy art for our home, pursue a career in interior decorating, volunteer for the board of directors of the local art museum, cultivate friendships with artists, or become a fund-raiser for artistic groups. Regardless of the outlet we choose, what's important is our willingness to provide an avenue of expression for our passion.

So now comes the question: What are you passionate about? If you can answer it, great. If you need more guidance to find the answer, try the following activities.

Divide a sheet of paper in half lengthwise. At the top of the left column, write the question, "What do I care most about in my life?" Jot down as many responses as you can think of. At the top of the right column, write the question, "What do I want for myself?" Answer in as many ways as you can. Now compare the two lists. The common responses indicate your passions.

Or try this activity with a different approach:

Suppose you have just been told that for five minutes next Saturday morning everyone in the world will stop what they're doing and listen to you. A satellite hookup will link everyone through television or radio so they can hear you. (Don't get distracted if you are afraid of public speaking. Just imagine that someone else will read what you write.) What would you say to a listening world? What have you learned that you want others to know?

Take some time right now to write out the four to seven things most important to you that you want to tell to other people. Remember, you've only got five minutes in which to talk, so you need to be succinct.

After you've finished writing, take a moment to review it. What are the most important things to you? These are your passions.

Discovering our passions is one step toward living more creatively. But the real adventure begins as you develop ways to communicate your passion. Your creativity will have an avenue of expression and you'll find yourself increasingly enthusiastic. Giving your passions a voice will enhance your motivation to take risks and to continue developing your creativity.

Anger: Creativity's Wrecking Ball

Anger can be both powerful and frightening. I don't know of any woman who, in her striving to become self-defined, hasn't confronted her rage. This is healthy. Becoming skilled in using anger constructively provides us with a previously untapped source of power. But until we reach this level of ability, anger can wreak havoc with our lives and our creativity.

It's easy for women to be angry. Jungian psychologist Irene Claremont de Castillejo suggests that deep within women's unconscious lies an unrecognized rage, passed from woman to woman over thousands of years—since civilization became an impersonal, unfeeling machine cutting us off from Nature, from our life force.[1]

Thinking of every woman inheriting anger passed through thousands of generations is staggering. But even if we doubt the notion of genetically based emotions, look at our own societal experience. Our holistic and feminine processes are generally dismissed. Our ideas are ignored or patronized. And all this happens before we've even finished second grade! Rage is a natural, healthy response in revolt to whatever separates us from ourselves. But when it buries itself deeply inside and has no constructive means of expression, anger becomes unhealthy.

In addition to the natural anger we all possess, we also have our life-specific reasons for accumulated anger, all of them equally justified. It may arise from childhood experiences of not being nurtured or recognized in ways meaningful to us. Other emotions such as fear, humiliation, or resentment are often channeled into anger. Regardless of its source, holding on to our anger is stagnating.

The Damage

Woman's psyche is founded on relatedness. The feminine experiences everything as connected to everything else. Our creativity often expresses itself in relationships in the home and on the job. But anger can destroy relationships. It separates us from other people who are intimidated by it or who don't want to be around it. It also damages our relationship with ourselves, especially our creativity. Unresolved anger cracks the foundation of our being.

Most coping methods we've learned for dealing with strong feelings have been unhealthy. We may explode with misdirected rage, becoming angry to a degree way out of proportion to the event. Fuming because we have to wait in line or yelling at another driver for something they've done wrong with their car are examples of misdirected rage. Many women stuff their anger so quickly they don't recognize this powerful emotion in themselves. Assertiveness training has helped, but we all know women who seethe under their carefully chosen words. Or we deliberately hold our anger inside, hoping it won't show. Because it has nowhere to go, it attacks our physical and emotional health instead. Internalized anger can lead to a variety of psychological problems, including depression. ◀

Unexpressed emotions can also give rise to many physical ailments, including intestinal problems, migraines, and even sinus infections! Louise Hay provides us with extensive insight into anger-related illnesses, including bursitis, bladder problems, earaches, gout, hemorrhoids,

See
Understanding the Creative/ Depressive Cycle
p. 97

hepatitis, pinkeye, plantar warts, and tetanus, among others.[2] Your body can probably provide you with its own list, which might include sore shoulders, general exhaustion, back problems, teeth grinding, or constant eyestrain.

Logic and reason don't compel us to reveal ourselves through the creative act—feelings do. But rage detours the passage of the initial creation away from other emotions, and everything comes out angry. The poem nags, the song preaches. The message, however delivered, harangues rather than stimulates, and our creative products are predictable and boring. Developing creativity as an element in our maturation becomes stifled.

Positive Anger

We do have a few role models for using anger constructively. Think about the woman who finally reaches her limit with drug pushers trying to influence her children. She mobilizes others to run criminals out and make the neighborhood safe. Many consumer groups have been formed because someone became angry about how businesses treat their customers. Lives have been improved, laws changed, and governments peacefully toppled because someone directed outrage to a constructive end. Can you think of examples of using anger constructively in your own life?

In learning to use anger positively, acknowledging it and feeling OK with it are important. Anger by itself is all right. What we *do* with the emotion makes the difference in our well-being. This is an important distinction. Too many women are trapped by negative messages around feeling anger. Overcoming those admonitions and accepting our anger are critical steps toward nurturing the growth of our creative self. Messages telling us we should not feel or show anger come from people who are afraid of their anger or who want to keep us in a de-powered position. The most personally powerful women I know have a full awareness of their anger and are partners with it in developing a healthy lifestyle.

The first step in learning how to use anger in positive ways is to recognize the emotion. Many of us are taught to deny it because being angry isn't "ladylike" or "nice." Living out this admonishment keeps us in denial. The following short activity is designed to help you bring an objective awareness to those incidents in your life which trigger your anger.

To help yourself recognize the situations which elicit an angry response, make a list of what makes you angry. Include situations as well as the things people say and do. If a seemingly little incident comes to mind, don't dismiss your feelings by saying, "Oh, I don't *really* get mad about that. It just irritates me a little." Small aggravations can add up to an emotional explosion. Awareness is the first step. Expression is the second.

Sometimes women fear the intensity of anger. A client expressed a common concern when she said, "I'm afraid if I let myself feel all this anger, I'll just explode. Or I'll be overwhelmed and disappear." I know of no cases where this fear has manifested itself, but it can be strong enough to keep someone from expressing her anger. Giving vent to stored emotions is a crucial step in clearing psychological baggage and turning the negative into the positive. The aid of a therapist can be beneficial, providing you with a safe place for feeling and expressing your emotions. Or you can try any or all of the following:

- Write in your journal
- Beat a rolled-up newspaper on pillows or a bed

- Yell from the tips of your toes inside a walk-in closet or closed car or outside in an open field.

While these last two suggestions can aid in releasing anger, they usually do nothing to help an individual resolve the cause or provide a positive channel. Nevertheless, they may be a necessary step in the process of finding a constructive expression for the rage.

Also be aware that explosions of anger disrupt the body's energy fields, leaving you unprotected and vulnerable.[3] So if you need to experience your anger in volatile ways such as yelling or beating a pillow, be certain to center yourself afterward, using the following activity.

~~~

Focus on your breathing, following your breath in, then following it out. Do this for several minutes until you feel calm and your attention is on your breathing. Now expand your awareness to include your entire body and the space one or two feet around it. Affirm that your energies are being brought back into alignment. You might say something like, "All my energy systems are perfectly aligned in and around my body." You may feel a tingling sensation or a sense of peace overcoming you as your energies shift into place. This important step keeps you balanced and protected from others' anger or negativity.

Using the Energy Constructively

Anger contains tremendous energy, so using it constructively means harnessing that force. What we're striving for is feeling the power in anger without being distracted by the emotion itself. Most of us are quite adept at mulling over incidents that made us angry. But doing that keeps us hooked into the emotion. Think about how you feel, how your body feels, when you're angry, paying particular attention to the strength and power of the energy. You might feel a rush of energy while your muscles tense. Learning to use this energy will enable you to make changes to benefit yourself.

An excellent guide in this process is your own health and well-being. In any situation where you find yourself becoming angry, ask yourself, "What can I do right now to keep myself healthy?" or "What is a healthy response for me right now?" When you allow yourself to be motivated by a desire to make healthy choices, you can use the anger energy to move forward, to take action. You might express your needs to someone else instead of allowing yourself to be dismissed. Now you're controlling the anger rather than it controlling you. And you're using the energy to motivate you to do something that might otherwise be nearly impossible.

At the same time, you're moving the anger energy rather than hanging on to it, thus freeing it for creative works. You'll have a new source of tremendous energy. Coming up with a creative idea is one thing, but having the energy and motivation to make it manifest requires a very different kind of effort. Freed anger directed toward a constructive end enables you to exert the effort required in a lot of creative endeavors.

Your relations with yourself and others will also grow clearer as you guide yourself by making healthy decisions. Your access to your creativity will become easier. You'll have a full range of feelings to connect with your creative inspiration. Naturally, these changes don't happen overnight. They take place gradually, with attention and a desire to use anger constructively. You may need to remind yourself frequently that you are now using anger energy to motivate yourself to achieve better health and increased creativity. That's OK.

With persistence, the experience of the pure energy will become natural, replacing feelings of destructive anger. These efforts retrain the body and repattern the mind. Once this happens, we naturally find ways to express our anger in positive ways. We may still become angry about certain things, but what we do with the anger will be different.

After diligent effort in this area, one client reported that she now gets angry less frequently. "It used to be that I would get angry and stuff it," she said. "Then I learned to take action as a result of my feelings. Now I find myself taking action without getting angry. I can fix a situation and never feel angry about it. This gives me a lot more energy for doing other things in my life!"

Sixty years ago author Virginia Woolf lamented the loss of creatively gifted women, their genius squandered in a morass of uncontrolled anger and bitterness.[4] The threat remains. But now we know how to transform a potentially stifling emotion into a powerful asset to our creative energy.

Altering Your Sense of Time

Nature marks the passage of time by certain events—sunrises, sunsets, tides, solstices. While these phenomena are predictable, they don't always happen at precisely the same time as measured by the clock. Nature experiences time fluidly, one event growing out of another. With our intimate ties to Nature, women also have a fluid sense of time. Rather than the masculine perception of time as linear and fragmented, we experience time cyclically and subjectively.[1] This perspective has implications for both our creativity and our time management.

During the creative process, time often becomes distorted. The creator may experience four hours as if they were a half hour, or half an hour may seem like four hours. You've probably experienced working intently on a project feeling as if you had worked a long time, only to suddenly realize very little "clock time" had passed. This phenomenon explains why creative works can sometimes be completed in a relatively short period of time. Some writers and artists have been so prolific that questions have been raised about whether they could have created so much by themselves. Given the nature of subjective time as experienced during the creative process, one person can accomplish a great deal in a short amount of objective time. And we can control this phenomenon, using it to our advantage.

Because women, through our feminine aspect, naturally have a continuous sense of time, we can easily alter our sense of clock time. And we can use this ability in our creative endeavors as well as in other areas of our lives. For instance, when we have to complete a lot of work in a short amount of time, we can work with an expanded sense of clock time to accomplish more than we normally could. The activity for making this shift may seem strange, but it's very effective. One client, a consultant with "never enough hours in the day," said of this technique, "It's completely changed how I work. I'm more efficient *and* more relaxed. What a combination!"

Seat yourself comfortably in a place where you'll be uninterrupted for at least ten minutes. Close your eyes. Imagine as vividly as possible a clock face without hands. See the numbers clearly starting with the number 12 at the top and the number 1 down and to the right, through the number 11 below and to the left of the 12. Look at each number separately, then look at the whole clock.

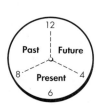

Now focus on the space from 12 to 4. Imagine that this section of the clock represents future time. You might even see the word *future* written beside the numbers. Now focus on the numbers from 4 to 8. This span represents present time. Label it *present*. Finally, look at the space from 8 to 12. This stands for past time. Mark it *past*. Your clock is now evenly divided among future, present, and past time.

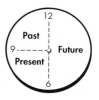

Now you're going to alter your sense of time using your clock. Focus again on the space between 12 and 4—future time. Expand this space so the future takes up the space from 12 to 6. The present is now from 6 to 9 and the past from 9 to 12. The future occupies half your sense of time. Now let the future return to its original position so future, present, and past take equal parts of the clock face.

Now focus on present time, which ranges from 4 to 8. Expand your sense of present time so it occupies the space from 2 to 10. The future now takes up the space from 12 to 2 and the past is from 10 to 12. The present takes most of your sense of time. Now let the present return to an equal portion of the clock face once again so future, present, and past are balanced.

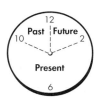

Now shift your attention to the past, the space from 8 to 12. Expand the past so it occupies the space from 6 to 12. The future and the present are evenly divided, with the future from 12 to 3 and the present from 3 to 6. Now let the past return to its original position again so future, present, and past are balanced on the clock face.

Now open your eyes and bring your attention to yourself and the room you're in.

Keeping Your Own Time

Play with shifting the numbers until you're comfortable with expanding and contracting time. With minimal practice you can do this easily. Then, depending on the task at hand, you can use this skill to increase your efficiency, your creativity, or your enjoyment of an event.

For example, if you have a lot of work to complete in a limited amount of time, begin by picturing your clock face. See the future, present, and past equally spaced on the clock. Then expand present time just as you did in the previous activity so it occupies the space between 2 and 10. Now open your eyes and begin your work.

With this altered sense of time, you'll find yourself able to accomplish more in less time as measured by a "real" clock. You will have more time for being creative, generating possibilities, exploring options, and combining ideas. By expanding the present, you've "tricked" yourself into believing you have more time than the clock indicates. When you're finished with your work, close your eyes and visualize the clock once again. Return the present time to its original position so future, present, and past occupy the same amount of space. If you forget to balance the three, you'll find that everything you do, like driving home or standing in line at the grocery store, will seem as if it's taking forever! Also, as tempting as it may be, resist using an expanded present for the entire working day. If you were to work under this condition day after day, you would run the risk of quickly burning yourself out. So use this technique only for those activities during the day for which you most need it.

You can improve your problem-solving abilities by extending your sense of future time, giving you greater access to future possibilities. Remind yourself of Nature's perspective—that time is fluid, with past, present, and future interconnected. Next, assure yourself that at some future point you have resolved this issue. As before, start this visualization with the clock evenly divided among the future, present, and past. Only this time, expand the future so it occupies the space from 12 to 6, then open your eyes and begin your work. This shift takes you out of the present, where the problem has not been solved, and moves you into the future, where it has been resolved. It gives you the new perspective needed for creative work. Make certain to balance the three time concepts at the conclusion of the task.

Expansion of the past has more recreational applications than everyday uses. For example, while exploring the old cathedrals of Cologne,

Germany, and a Mayan temple in Belize, I used an expanded sense of the past. This heightened my sensitivity to these ancient structures, their stories, and their people, enriching my experience. History students might be more enthusiastic about the subject if they studied it with an expanded sense of the past. As with the other activities, when you use this technique, return your clock face to a balance among the three times. Otherwise you'll have a vague sense of having left something behind somewhere.

By relaxing into our feminine aspect with its fluid sense of time and using the technique of time expansion, we become more creative as problem-solvers and more efficient at the same time! We can use a phenomenon which frequently occurs during the creative process to enhance our work lives. Or we can consciously alter our sense of time to improve our creative output.

&xpanding Your
Sense of Self

An artist tells me she can paint for hours without stopping, even forgetting to eat. "Where are you mentally when you allow this to happen?" I ask. "I don't really know. I don't feel like I'm in my studio or even in Tucson. It's a different reality."

Most of us have had this sense of being lost in time, focusing all our attention on a project and suddenly looking at a clock or being interrupted by someone and finding to our amazement that much more (or less) time has passed than we thought. This phenomenon is common during the creative process. ◀ But sometimes when we are in a highly creative state, we lose a lot more than our sense of time. We also lose our sense of self. That's how the artist can forget to eat.

That part of ourselves which is concerned with mundane tasks like eating, cleaning, washing clothes, paying bills, and buying groceries is the "little local self." While it handles many basic necessities, it can also keep us stuck in routine. Its vision is limited. When we're trapped in our little local self we can't see the interconnections between us and all other things. From this perspective we are likely to attempt solving a problem at the level of the problem instead of changing our perspective to get to the core issue. ▶ Our creative possibilities are virtually nonexistent.

See
**Altering
Your Sense
of Time**
p. 119

See
**Becoming a
Creative
Problem-Solver**
p. 135

When we lose ourselves in the moment of creation, like the artist I described above, we shift out of an awareness of our ordinary selves and move into an expanded realm. In this state, tapping into our creative potential is easier. Unfortunately, the expectations placed on women can make it hard to move beyond our little local selves into more creative states. We are still in charge of the routine tasks in the home, getting the children where they need to be when they need to be there, and supporting everyone's emotional needs.

Moving into New States of Awareness

See
**Becoming
More
Spontaneous**
p. 165

Being overly focused on routine activities like these stifles creativity. ▶ The importance of breaking out of burdensome routines becomes exaggerated when we look at the need to grow out of our little local self. By devoting blocks of time to our creative endeavors, we encourage shifting to a new level, a different perspective, an enlarged sense of self operating beyond the ordinary.

From our expanded self we gain a sense of being part of the larger whole, where we can access creative possibilities. We have moved out of our ordinary state of consciousness into an altered one. There's nothing spooky or mysterious about being in a nonordinary state of awareness. We do it all day long. We drive to work but can't recall the details of the experience. Or we drift off into some unknown place only to be brought back to reality by the sudden realization that we can't remember what happened during the last several minutes.

Virginia Woolf talked about this phenomenon in women: "Again if one is a woman one is often surprised by a sudden splitting off of consciousness . . . . Clearly the mind is always altering its focus and bringing the world into different perspectives."[1]

We can use this natural ability to our benefit. By deliberately shifting out of an ordinary state of consciousness, we leave behind our little local self with its restricted vision and open ourselves to creative realms. Creativity generally occurs in nonordinary states of awareness. Some unusual methods have been used to accomplish this change.[2] Descartes would wrap himself in blankets and sit by a fire, secreting great works. Alcohol and drugs have long been used to disinhibit consciousness, eventually causing destruction of skill, talent, and creative potential. Apparently, the onset of tuberculosis releases toxins into the brain which stimulate creativity. Remember all those tubercular British writers? I don't recommend any of these methods.

I began exploring various brain-wave states in the mid-'70s, first doing guided imagery, then trance work. While my experience taught me these shifts are relatively easy to accomplish, many "experts" warned about the difficulties of achieving certain brain-wave states. I am surprised by how many people still believe it is difficult.

Consciousness is always changing. Our brain understands and is comfortable with different states of consciousness. All we need to do is ask our brain to shift, then wait calmly for a response. The more we practice, the easier it becomes to move to the desired state.

We generally talk about four brain-wave states—*beta*, the waking state; *alpha*, a relaxed meditative state; *theta*, a deep trance state; *delta*, a sleeping state. This is a highly simplified model. I've experienced numerous states within each of these, especially alpha and theta, but I don't have the language to name each of them. For our purposes, focusing on these four will suffice. Creative expression often occurs in the alpha or theta states.

The following activity, extracted from a Jean Houston/Robert

Masters exercise, is designed to help you attune yourself to these brain-wave states and communicate with your brain to achieve them. This activity simply asks you to bring awareness to something you've probably done several times already today! It should be done in a quiet place where you won't be interrupted.

Seated in a comfortable position, center yourself by focusing your attention on your breathing, following it in and out. Do this for a few minutes.

Now shift your attention to your brain. Remind yourself that this marvelous organ understands various brain-wave states and knows how to move easily from one to the other.

Begin by asking your brain to emit beta waves so you feel alert and fully awake. Repeat the phrase "beta waves" several times. Now ask your brain to emit alpha waves, a calmer wave leaving you feeling relaxed and meditative. Repeat the words "alpha waves" until you feel a change. Feel the shift in your body. Your breathing will slow somewhat. Your muscles will feel relaxed. A sense of calm may envelop you.

Now ask your brain to emit theta waves—slow, trance-inducing waves. Theta waves, theta waves, theta waves. Now your body will feel more deeply relaxed. You could lift your arm only by using a lot of effort. Your breathing is slower and your entire being feels very calm.

Now ask your brain to emit delta waves so you feel drowsy and could easily fall asleep. Delta waves bring you very close to the total relaxation of deep sleep.

Now ask for beta waves again, bringing you to a full waking state. Repeat the cycle several times to become familiar with each state.

As you take yourself through this activity, allow adequate time to feel the difference with each change in brain wave. But don't let yourself fall asleep in delta! Take yourself through the four states several times so you can gain a clear distinction between each and be comfortable with the shift. The more you practice with varying your brain-wave states, the easier it will be for you to shift to alpha or theta as you're working on creative projects. You can accomplish this sitting at your desk, in front of the computer, in your studio, or wherever you do your creative work. Simply ask your brain to shift you to an alpha or theta state, then begin creating. In these relaxed states, ideas can flow and parts of the brain not accessible in a normal waking state are opened.

In the theta state, we may even be tapping into a band of pure creative energy, the source of the self-creating work of art that seems to form itself. Barbara Mettler, internationally known for her work in creative movement improvisation, describes herself as an instrument through which creativity is poured. Creative people who encourage this flow often report feeling as if they weren't creating the work but are merely the vehicle for its transmission. Musicians hear their music before it's written. Writers laugh at things characters in their novels say and do, hearing and seeing the action for the first time as it's written. But this level of creativity isn't available to us in our ordinary state of consciousness or while we're trapped in our little local self. As we alter our brain-wave state and expand out of our routine self, we open to these extended creative potentials.

These experiences are open to all of us, not just artists. The following describes what happened to a management consultant who had to present the results of an extensive study of employees to the managers of the company. Since the findings were critical of the existing culture and management, she was apprehensive about the presentation.

She described herself as

> *Physically exhausted, emotionally ragged, suffering from jet lag and with no idea how I was going to make it through the next hour. Then as I got into the presentation, I began to hear myself making statements and drawing connections that hadn't occurred to me when I was preparing my notes . . . . It was my mouth moving, but the words and thoughts were someone else's. I remember thinking as I sat down afterwards, 'Gee, what a great presentation. I wonder who gave it?' The feedback from the audience was gratifying; they accepted the findings, appreciated the counsel, and seemed prepared to take positive action. . . . But there was also relief at my first experience with what I've since come to think as the Creative Self, the reassurance of a higher wisdom ready to play a role if given the opportunity.*

Creative possibilities may also open to us in a hyperalerted beta state, which is achieved by asking the brain to make such a shift, or through exercise quickly pumping a lot of oxygen into the brain. ▶ This amounts to a controlled super-awake state, deliberately induced to stimulate creative efforts. Once the goal is achieved, I recommend resuming a more ordinary state. Regularly attempting to accomplish a great deal in a hyperalerted state can lead to burnout.

Letting Nature Help

Our close ties to Nature can teach us to be comfortable with shifting our state of consciousness. The activity described in "Understanding Your Feminine Nature" ◀ is designed to guide you to an experience of being at one with Nature, without boundaries between you and everything in Nature. In this state, your little local self is left behind as you

See
Dancing with Goliath
p. 241

See
Understanding Your Feminine Nature
p. 39

expand your sense of self, gaining greater access to creative energies. In addition to the activity already described, you can accomplish a feeling of being part of nature using this Zen walking meditation:

> Take yourself outdoors, preferably to a place where you are standing on grass or dirt rather than concrete. Now simply concentrate on your feet as they touch the ground. Take one step slowly and deliberately, focusing your attention on each part of your foot as it first leaves then contacts the earth. As your foot moves down to touch the earth, imagine the ground reaching up to contact your foot. Sense the two merging as you walk so you can't tell where your foot ends and the ground begins. Now allow this sensation of being one with Nature to infuse your whole body. You might find yourself taking five minutes to cover a distance that would normally take as little as thirty seconds. This is an extremely slow, deliberate experience.
>
> When you take some time during the day for this activity, you'll feel renewed and invigorated and be in touch with creative energies. By leaving your little local self, you'll shift perspectives on a challenging problem, feeling relaxed and centered, seeing the old in new ways.

The point of this activity and the brain-wave exercise earlier in the chapter is to allow yourself to experience a different state of awareness, moving out of the ordinary, becoming comfortable with nonordinary states conducive to creative work. As you learn to orchestrate these changes, you'll learn which ones are most helpful to you in your creative work. And you'll be able to call upon the appropriate shift in consciousness when and where you need it.

Part Three
Integrating Creativity into Your Daily Life

Becoming a Creative Problem-Solver

Six department heads sitting at a table—stuck. Our weekly staff meeting had been told that a senior executive was transferring. In keeping with company tradition, each division was to design a comedy skit to present at his farewell party. This should have been fun, but as the group rejected one idea after another, the mood turned negative, effectively stopping all creative efforts.

In an attempt to change both the atmosphere and the lack of creativity, I suggested looking at the executive's new workplace. From this perspective, we could find unique features about the new site and play up those in the skit. This shift worked. Lifted from our immediate surroundings, we mentally transported ourselves several thousand miles away. We quickly found numerous things to satirize. Our creativity was revitalized, the mood of the meeting changed, and we outlined the skit in a short time. By shifting out of the level of the problem—in this case literally envisioning a different physical location—we gained a new perspective. Everyone easily joined in, welcoming the freshness of the variation and having fun with the task.

Regardless of the seriousness of the project, a change in how the problem is perceived can make all the difference in arriving at viable solutions. Attempting to solve an issue at the level of the problem inevitably results in more problems, whereas by moving to a different level of the problem, we can address its root cause.[1] Unfortunately, most of us have participated in meetings where the focus of our problem-solving efforts stayed at the level of the problem. Our endeavors may have resulted in a "Band-Aid solution" that sooner or later became another problem because we treated the symptoms, not the problem, and failed to examine the potential consequences of our "solution." Sound familiar?

When we make holistic thinking a part of the problem-solving process, we can prevent the "Band-Aid solution" dilemma. Our holistic thinking facilitates making mental leaps from one point to another without following a rigid pattern. It enables us to associate apparent opposites in arriving at a unique and final solution to a problem. By calling on these characteristics of holistic thinking, we can see a problem from new perspectives, from different levels.

Holistic thinking can easily be incorporated into problem-solving. For example, using imagery at different stages of the process guides us into the realms of holistic thinking and opens the way for shifts to a different level of experiencing the problem. Ideally, the final step in problem-solving is the evaluation of the outcome. This can also be an appropriate time for a change in perspective. Normally, the business world determines the success or failure of a project by how close it comes to a preset outcome. If the desired result was accomplished, the project is deemed a success. If the goal wasn't realized, the venture is judged a failure. This latter determination can be damaging to morale and the desire to tackle new projects in the future. Strict adherence to initial goals leads to mediocrity. A process-oriented perspective, on the other hand, defines a project's success by how open it is to fulfilling its own potential. Making the final evaluation from this different perspective can turn an apparent failure into a success.

For example, 3M managed such a shift several years ago at the conclusion of a project aimed at developing the latest version of a super-glue.[2] After months of research that cost millions of dollars, researchers failed to create the desired outcome. The end product wasn't super-glue, but the substance produced did possess some peculiar properties. It stuck but didn't stick. When evaluated according to the stated purpose of the research, the entire project was a failure.

But one scientist shifted to a different level—a new way of viewing the project and its outcome. When he evaluated the new product in terms of its useful properties, he realized that 3M had created an enormous success. By discovering the possibilities for their failed super-glue, 3M devised a completely new and very useful product. Now no office can function without Post-it™ Note Pads, those "little yellow stickies" that stick but don't stick.

A variety of techniques can stimulate a shift away from the level of the problem, starting with awareness. By reminding ourselves that a problem can't be solved at the level of the problem, we can keep alert to the phenomenon. While distilling the issue down to a simple statement, we should frequently ask ourselves, "How can I see this issue from another perspective?" If the problem-solving process becomes bogged down, we can examine what's happening or not happening by challenging ourselves to shift to a different level.

Something as basic as sitting in the same place for a long period of time can dull the problem-solving effort. The issue being discussed becomes strongly associated with the physical space. This connection needs to be broken for the participants to become creative in their approach. Taking a break to move around, then returning to a different seat encourages a fresh view of the problem. Or the entire group may benefit from moving to a new room or even outdoors. Remember the last time you felt stuck in the same place, grinding away at an issue? Moving helps!

Brainstorming is a frequently used technique for stimulating creativity. Unfortunately, it's often used incorrectly. People want to skim over this process, not giving it enough time to be effective. Remember the ground rules for productive brainstorming.

All ideas are acceptable—the more outrageous, the better. None are dismissed. Each suggestion should be written where all participants can see it. The leader should encourage everyone to become ridiculous and even silly. Creative inspiration, *aha!*, is one step from *ha-ha*. When working alone on a project, laughing out loud at this state indicates you're on the right track. The further you can stretch the limit of possibilities, even to the absurd, the more potential solutions you'll have available. And generate lots of possible solutions—at least ten for each participant. A group of ten people should come up with a minimum of one hundred suggestions. Most brainstorming sessions fall far short of this number. The creative juices need priming before they start flowing.

Consulting with a child problem-solver is also helpful. She or he can generate solutions free from adult biases. While it's unlikely that your workplace has this young consultant, you can confer with your own children or nieces and nephews. Better yet, you can find this child within yourself. Ask her how she would cope with the issue. You'll have to suspend much of your adult thinking, especially judgments, to hear what she has to say. The most creative adults usually have many childlike (not child*ish*) qualities allowing for fresh perspectives and insights needed in problem-solving. Many activities in this book stimulate the creative inner child so you can call on her for help in resolving a dilemma.

Another method of shifting perspectives requires newsprint and colored pencils or crayons. Each participant in the problem-solving session draws the problem, either abstractly or literally. Those who have inhibitions about drawing may need to be encouraged. Using the non-dominant hand to quickly create an abstract representation of the problem can break through many blocks, as can drawing with eyes closed so you don't look at your picture until you're finished. These drawings should be completed in five to ten minutes, with as little conscious thought going into them as possible. Then explain your drawing to the other participants.

Next, the discussion focuses on how the problem as represented in each drawing can be resolved. The idea is to devise solutions for each picture or for parts of the picture, incorporating many suggestions into the drawing itself. The best proposals can form the basis for a plan to resolve the problem.

Another effective method of shifting perspectives is *guided imagery*. The destination of this imaginary journey is a place in nature where a solution to the problem can be found. This session should be led by a group member with an especially soothing voice. The instructions for the imagery session might sound like this:

> Begin by closing your eyes and focusing on your breathing. Follow the breath in as you inhale, and follow it out as you exhale. Do this for ten breaths.
>
> Let your breathing return to normal.
>
> Now see and feel yourself walking in the woods. You're just strolling leisurely on a clearly marked path, feeling the soft dirt beneath your feet. Smelling the fresh air. Watching the sun flit through the trees. The temperature is just right, very comfortable for a walk in the woods. Listen for the sounds around you—birds singing, a squirrel scampering up a tree, the breeze rustling the leaves.
>
> As you're walking in these woods, you become aware

that there is a special quality about this place. This is where questions are answered, problems solved, secrets revealed. The place where you now find yourself will reveal the resolution to the problem we've been working on. (At this point, the leader should restate the problem.) Continuing to walk, or stopping to rest on a log or rock, invite the answer to the problem. (Allow several minutes of silence.)

Sometimes Nature gives us answers in somewhat abstract ways. If she does that with you now, ask for more information about what you're being given so you clearly understand how it relates to the problem. (Allow about five minutes of silence.)

It's time now to return to the room, bringing with you the information you received about the problem we've been working on. But before you leave the woods, thank it for providing you with guidance. Now gradually return your awareness to the room, focusing on your breathing and coming to full alertness in five breaths. The first deep breath begins bringing you back to the room. With the second breath you're becoming aware of yourself seated in the room. The third breath carries you half-way back. The fourth breath brings you almost to a full waking state. Now you're fully awake and alert on the fifth breath.

Next, the group discusses what each participant learned from this experience. Everyone describes her experience in detail. Even if someone doesn't understand what she saw or thinks the imagery was irrelevant, the experience needs to be shared. Some people in the group may find meaning where others don't. Concepts and solutions should be discussed openly with every idea encouraged. Only after everyone has presented her experience should solutions be analyzed for effectiveness. No idea, no matter how remote it seems, should be rejected without consideration. A solution that appears obtuse to one participant may be absolutely clear to another. Or it may stimulate someone else into coming up with the perfect resolution. The leader must be careful to keep the discussion open and free of judgments while involving everyone equally.

I admit that some of these activities may seem unusual, but they effectively accomplish a shift away from perceiving the problem at the level of the problem. They stimulate the creative process, allowing for truly innovative solutions. Moving out of the level at which the problem occurs becomes as easy as riding an elevator from one floor to the next.

Honoring the Unmeasurable

The idea that a tangible product must result from creative expression dominates our concept of what is creative. The painting, the book, or the scientific discovery are easy to measure or put a price tag on. In the second chapter of this book, "Getting Down to the Roots: What Is Creativity?" you were encouraged to come up with your definition of creativity. And you were urged to consider the intangible products of your creative process, especially in the realm of relationships. Women often express creativity intangibly.

But acknowledging and rewarding intangible products is difficult because they are often subjective in their influence and don't lend themselves to simple measurement. For example, when we mold co-workers' energy into a productive group, we're exercising our unique creative talent. The family as a cohesive unit would not exist without our skills involving relationships. But creative acts such as these are hard to recognize and reward. Let's take a closer look at how we can acknowledge our intangible products.

Creativity in Relationships

American business, classrooms, and homes critically need the conscious exercise of our creativity in relationships. And the first step toward using this inherent ability is recognizing and validating the creative effort required.

I'm not saying that all women always build healthy relationships. We know that's not true. But remember what the goddesses show us about our feminine natures—by expressing this natural aspect of ourselves, we can develop and maintain constructive relationships. ◀ Like any talent, this ability needs cultivating.

See
Understanding Your Feminine Nature
p. 39

Historically, we've had generations of practice orchestrating relationships that require blending many complex factors. An obvious example of this is giving a dinner party. I know, some of you may be saying to yourselves, "Who cares about a dinner party? I do more than that." But that's exactly my point: I want to honor the creativity that happens in the home because it shouldn't be ignored or trivialized any longer. The dinner party, something common to most of us, illustrates our ability to pull together varying elements and create a positively functioning whole. But we're often the first to dismiss the creativity involved. So, for now, let's consider the dinner party.

Usually we start our planning by thinking about the guests' personalities and deciding who will get along with whom. The complexities of the human personality make this aspect of the project the most complicated. Only after we've satisfied ourselves that the guests selected will provide a positive and stimulating mix do we arrive at an invitation list.

Next, we plan the menu. Here we're relating foods to guarantee the entire meal is compatible for tastes, textures, nutrition, and appearance. All this time, we're seeing and tasting the meal in our imagination, making adjustments according to how we experience the total effect, and using our imagery to juggle many combinations.

Finally, the party itself takes place. All our efforts come together as we stimulate interaction among the guests while timing various parts of the meal, ensuring the entire event runs smoothly and enjoyably. When everyone has gone, we're exhausted from all this orchestrating. And our husbands or partners, giving us an appreciative kiss, comment that we ought to do this more often. After all, it looks so effortless!

As women left the home to pursue other careers, we took all these creative abilities with us. We use them every day, no matter what our profession. But we often fail to appreciate or appropriately value these creative talents. Think about your job and the ways in which you use your creativity.

One example is developing a positive, productive work atmosphere. In recent years the business world has begun paying more attention to how the workplace environment influences productivity. Simply put, a positive environment leads to high productivity while a negative one drags it down. Although each worker influences the prevailing ambiance, the most pervasive control comes from the person in charge—the supervisor, the head of the department, or the general manager. The management style of this individual, her willingness to deal with conflict, and her attitude toward work and her employees all set the tone for the total environment. She can consciously develop a positive atmosphere by using the same creative expertise she uses to hostess a dinner party—only in business it's called team building.

The person in charge needs to be aware that her personality strongly influences the prevailing group feeling. The supervisor (or teacher or . . .) can easily project feelings such as anger, frustration, or stress into the workplace, making the atmosphere negative for everyone. Conversely, her sense of calm during a crisis or her overall positive attitude help create a constructive ambiance enhancing productivity and creativity. The effective female manager creates the environment she wants by modeling the desired feelings and behaviors. Even if you're not the boss, you can contribute to a positive situation by developing a productive working rapport with your peers and supervisor. One person can have a significant effect upon the ambiance in any setting.

A word of caution: establishing this atmosphere may mean fine-tuning your own relationship skills. You'll have to face any co-dependent issues you may have with others. Workaholics and perfectionists must confront their addictions and learn constructive ways of experiencing work and co-workers. ◀

Also remember that awakening creative energies in one area stimulates creativity in other realms. So the feminine's ability to nurture relationships will unfold as we expand our creative expression. In the meantime, we no longer need to be restricted to limited ideas of creative expression. Validating our intangible products nurtures our creative self. This important link is reflected in a comment made by Portia Nelson, actress, author, and painter:

> " *I* feel like creativity *is* my life . . . and by the same token, *life* is creativity. It's the only way I know to live . . . and by that I mean . . . I do so many different things I'm always into some creative endeavor . . . . I do feel all creative areas are connected to each other in some way. At least, for me, one seems to trigger another. "

See
Perfectionism: Creativity's Saboteur
p. 89

$\mathcal{R}$edefining Power

Traditionally women have led society in the direction of personal development. We seek professional help with personal issues more often than men do. Growth-oriented workshops usually have more women than men in attendance. I'm not suggesting that women are obligated to be the leaders in the area of growth, but if we do have a natural inclination toward self-improvement, we can use it to our advantage. As we learn healthier ways to manage ourselves, we also discover improved skills for managing others. But on this journey, everything we do ought to empower us as individuals and encourage us to use our power over ourselves.

Nurturing ourselves leads us to an increased awareness of *self-power*. The therapy we choose, the workshops we attend, the books we read, should all empower us to find our direction, our sense of inner self. We're creating ourselves. Too often, however, the therapy, workshop, or book takes power away from us by persuading us to accept someone else's process or to adopt an outside notion of how we should define ourselves. While empowerment is the ideal, many people and situations exist to help us accomplish the opposite.

Empowering Ourselves

One way we de-power ourselves is by striving to become "normal." I once taught a college class called "Normal Personality," a remarkable topic since there's no such thing as a normal person. I used Jean Houston's definition of a normal person—someone you don't know very well.[1] Yet too many therapies endeavor to make everyone's behavior "normal," smoothing and soothing all the rough edges out of life. This striving toward comfortable sameness also removes all creative possibilities. Creativity arises from the fringes of our lives, from the questions we have about our behavior or perceptions, and from challenges to the status quo. If the therapy fails to stimulate these questions and help us discover the answers within ourselves, then it's detracting from our growth as self-defined women.

We give our power away when we allow a therapist to interpret our dreams for us or when we go along with a medical doctor telling us we must do what she or he says without adequate explanation. We reclaim our power by working with therapists who guide us on our individual path and by insisting on the explanations that help us understand ourselves. We avoid people who make decisions for us, who discount our ideas, feelings, and efforts.

Sometimes we give our power away by exercising poor self-management skills that interfere with living creatively. Failing to finish what we've started, waiting until the last minute to begin working on a project, refusing to take responsibility for our actions or inactions—all these behaviors undermine the creative process. By neglecting to complete projects, perhaps unloading them onto someone else when we become bored or discover we've started too many ventures, we give the message that we're unreliable. And we disappoint ourselves. The creativity we put into an endeavor will never be recognized if we hand over the task before completing it.

"I work better under pressure" is the usual excuse given for waiting until the last minute to start a project. We have all tried to work with people who insist on procrastination as a work style. They're very difficult to cope with, especially when part or all of our work depends on what they accomplish. This excuse often comes from people who are poor managers of themselves. They tend to be disorganized and their work shows little originality because it's completed in haste. Certainly creative ideas have to incubate, but they also need time to be expressed, explored, and refined. Someone caught in the habit of waiting until the last minute needs to pace herself. She needs to manage her time efficiently and be accountable to her co-workers for inconveniences she causes them with her lack of constructive self-management skills.

Accountability for our actions or inactions is tied to responsibility—or being response-able. Too often, the word *responsible* carries burdensome overtones of the shoulds and have tos that interfere with spontaneity. But if we break it down, the word becomes response-able, in other words, able to respond to a situation from a variety of possibilities. We have choices in our behavior. Herein lies a key element in self-power. We're responsible when we're able to respond to people and situations and life. We no longer react (re-act), repeating the same inhibiting behaviors over and over. We exercise choices in our actions and take credit for the fruits of our creativity. Similarly, our accountability for our role in a failed project enables us to work toward a more positive resolution. We don't get stuck in looking for someone to blame for a "failure." And we don't take total liability when it doesn't belong to us. We accept our part and contribute to as constructive an outcome as possible.

We can all devise many mismanagement techniques that keep us from being as creative as we could be. Old habits may inhibit our growth, but they're often comfortable and not easily discarded. Sometimes we can accomplish changes in behavior by ourselves; sometimes we need the help of a therapist. Always our goal is to evolve into who we are, independent of societal and familial expectations—to become who we are as *we* choose to define ourselves. As we move in this direction, we can't help but become better at managing others. Empowerment is contagious.

Empowering Others

We empower others by encouraging them to make their own decisions, express their creative ideas, and pursue the development of their potential. We become the manager who looks for the best in our people and guides them in developing positive qualities. We assist an employee who's overcoming unproductive behaviors. As we break patterns of negative behavior—unhealthy people use bad habits as their excuse for not changing—we're modeling the kind of behavior we want in the workplace or home. This shouldn't be a burden. Enhancing our self-management skills so we become more creative ought to make our lives easier and less stressful.

Many of the techniques we can use to nurture our growth are also useful with others. Positive reinforcement is perhaps the simplest, most effective, yet frequently overlooked method for encouraging growth. The well-deserved recognition of a specific accomplishment improves morale and invites more quality work. I encourage clients to keep a record of how frequently they give constructive feedback to people in their lives as well as to themselves! These statements should combine sincerity with simplicity. A sentence or two referring to a specific activity, such as, "I like the way you conduct yourself at meetings. You're cooperative and helpful in keeping things moving," lets people know they're being paid attention to and their work is valuable. The same technique can be used by teachers with their students and mothers with their children. Co-workers can be supportive of each other by acknowledging each others' successes. When was the last time you recognized someone's creative effort?

Employees who are regularly supported in their positive behaviors are more likely to approach their manager with creative ideas. By giving attention and reinforcement to constructive actions, negative ones lose power. We can give this kind of support to those around us as well as to ourselves, empowering everyone toward a more creative lifestyle.

When women began assuming more management positions during the early '70s, our bosses often inadvertently inhibited our professional growth. They were reluctant to give us feedback about behaviors interfering with our advancement because they feared being accused of prejudice. Yet in order to grow everyone needs information about their behavior along with support for change. If we avoid giving feedback about unproductive work habits, we may sabotage both our employees and our effectiveness as a manager.

Feedback regarding someone's negative behavior should be guided by a definite goal, such as bringing about a positive change in work habits. By citing specific, concrete examples of the individual's negative behavior, we can assist the employee in recognizing the inappropriate behavior. For example, "You've been late three times this week. That's unacceptable." Separating the person and the behavior is also important. We're not telling the employee she or he is unacceptable—we're saying the behavior is.

During any discussion of negative behavior, positive strokes ought to be kept out. Mixing positive feedback with the negative is confusing and can have the effect of watering down the message that this person needs to change certain behaviors in order to perform better. A statement such as "I have confidence in you to improve in this area" reinforces chances of changed behavior. Most people respond well to feedback about their behavior when it's given with the intent of helping them improve.

While you may not have a manager's title, you undoubtedly have many areas in your life where you are managing: secretaries manage their work areas (and sometimes their bosses); teachers manage classrooms; nurses manage patients and their care; mothers manage homes, children, and (sometimes) a partner. Regardless of the specifics, the point remains the same. As we put forth the effort to reinforce the best in others and in ourselves, we encourage creativity. The work or home environment becomes a healthier, emotionally safer place where everyone can be uniquely themselves.

As we continue to grow as individuals, learning more about managing ourselves creatively, we can use our knowledge to enhance relations with our employees, students, peers, or children. During this process, we're drawn to anything and anyone encouraging our development and empowerment as individuals, while rejecting anything that de-powers us. We resist the "normalcy" that seeks to smooth out our creative rough edges. And we become more creative in our interactions with others. Our ability to manage others improves as we learn more about managing ourselves.

$\mathcal{E}$xercising Your Imagery

Our imagery is powerful. It can affect our bodies for both health and illness. Studies of successful people show they regularly imagine themselves already doing what they are striving to accomplish. The greater our skill with using different types of imagery, the more we open ourselves to creative possibilities. The human brain functions in images, so when we use our imagery, we exercise our brains and enhance our creativity.

Those of us who grew up in the '40s and '50s had to be sneaky about using our imagery. Psychologists believed that fantasizing playmates was unhealthy for us and that it would lead to confusion about what was real and what wasn't. We were admonished by parents and teachers to stop daydreaming, as if this, too, would lead to distorted development. But many of us persisted, learning when to bring out our pretend friends and when to keep them hidden. We kept our internal imagery alive while looking as if we were devotedly attentive to the teacher's every word. But the stories in our minds were usually more interesting than anything we read in school and more inventive than television and movies!

The '60s brought an explosion of brain research which helped change negative attitudes about using imagery. Now the importance of exercising our imaginations is more thoroughly understood. Virtually every creative act is sparked by some image. For women, something internal must happen to start the creative juices flowing. Sometimes the creator might experience an external image, such as a scene in nature or a verbal description, which hits her with enough force to grab her attention. Then she internalizes this impression, combining it with some inner image, and brings forth a new thought or feeling. If she's satisfied with this creation, she'll give it form according to her creative talents. Sound familiar?

Imagery Explained

Imagery is associated with the five senses. We can have visual (sight), auditory (hearing), kinesthetic (a feeling in the body, especially in the muscles), gustatory (tasting), and olfactory (smelling) imagery. Most people have a predominant type of imagery that is easiest for them to use. Auditory imagery is common among musicians while kinesthetic imagery frequently dominates among dancers and athletes. Many painters are visual imagers. But regardless of the primary imagery, we can develop skill in using other types.

When you work with imagery, it's important to honor what happens. For instance, if you see only blackness when you practice the activity at the end of this section, sensing the scene rather than visualizing it, you're responding kinesthetically. Don't berate yourself because you didn't see the image or because you heard it more clearly than you saw or felt it. As you work/play with your imagery, you increase the likelihood of fully developing all types of imagery, thereby gaining greater access to your creative possibilities.

Shifts from one type of imagery to another can sometimes be disquieting, as a workshop participant once experienced. She approached me after I led an exercise designed so each participant could experience her inner goddess. This woman was upset with herself because she decided she "blocked" the exercise. Her usually strong visual imagery wasn't operating—she saw nothing. Yet I noticed she wrote almost a full page of notes following the exercise. They revealed that indeed the woman had experienced a deep connection to a goddess; her impressions were actually quite clear. I explained that she perceived the exercise with her kinesthetic sense, feeling it with her body rather than seeing it. I congratulated her on acquiring a new closeness with this part of her inner self. She stopped belittling herself for "blocking" and began feeling good about what she accomplished.

The Power of Imagery

I first explored the power of imagery during training in psychosynthesis, a school of psychology that makes extensive use of guided fantasy during therapeutic situations. I was teaching high school English at the time and found the guided imagery activities especially helpful. While other teachers struggled to teach students how to write a descriptive paragraph, I took my students on guided fantasies where they could internally experience the story I was describing. I provided the outline while they filled in the details using their imagery. Or I described the beginning of a story and instructed them to finish it by themselves. By involving all their senses in the experience, they explored the richness of their imaginations, then wrote. The problem wasn't lack of descriptive detail, but rather enough class time to set it onto paper.

Another bonus to using imagery techniques in the classroom is that they increase students' repertoire of learning styles. What I mean is that our favored learning style parallels our dominant imagery. So if my predominant imagery is visual, I learn easiest when I see something. If it's auditory, I learn by hearing. As long as my learning style and the teaching style being used in the classroom coincide, I'm OK. But if I'm a visual learner with a teacher who relies on the auditory, I'm probably going to have problems. I may even be labeled a slow learner. But as I develop more types of imagery, I gain access to increased varieties of learning styles.

Many of my students were minorities: Mexican-American, African-American, Asian, and Native American. I found most didn't learn auditorially or visually, the way the dominant culture expected. Instead, they learned kinesthetically. Consequently, kinesthetic imagery was their dominant type. Once I began using guided fantasy activities which validated their favored type of imagery, they gained a new appreciation of themselves and their abilities.

I remember the wide-eyed excitement of one student who, for six months, experienced these exercises through his kinesthetic sense and then suddenly shifted to visual imagery. "I could see it!" he exclaimed. He expanded his inner world of imagery along with his outer world of learning.

Although imagery is associated with the five senses, researchers Stanislav Grof, Jean Houston, and Robert Masters discovered that imagery happens at varying depths within the human psyche.[1,2,3] Initially, four levels were uncovered. Grof, with his Freudian background, associated these levels with the birth trauma, while Houston and Masters connected them with types of experience.

For Houston and Masters, the first, the sensory level, arises from an individual's experience with the outside world, such as a painting that conveys the realism of a photograph. The second, the psychological level, is formed from an individual's experience with herself. The third layer is the mythological, with imagery taking on universal symbolism, such as mandalas and spirals which are found in cultures worldwide. Finally, the deepest level of imagery is the integral layer where all other levels are synthesized. It's the place where the individual experiences union with all-that-is. Grof, Houston, and Masters discovered that once a person genuinely experiences this fourth level, she gains access to universal wisdom and emerges a healthier, more integrated and well-balanced person. These feelings of cosmic unity parallel Abraham Maslow's descriptions of peak experiences in the self-actualized person.

Since her early research, Dr. Houston has found many layers within these layers. I remember a lengthy exercise in which she led workshop participants on an experience of over fifty levels of imagery!

So we carry within ourselves a rich vastness reached through our imagery. This wealth of inner knowing and experience contains the key to becoming creative, regardless of the application of the creativity. Certainly most challenges we meet creatively don't require a journey into the deepest part of our psyche. But knowing how to stimulate and use all types of imagery expands our repertoire and puts us in touch with our creative capabilities.

Learning to Use Imagery

Many of the activities in this book require using internal images. You can practice using your imagery in fun ways. For example, right now, close your eyes and recall your favorite meal. Smell the food. Look at it. Taste it, letting all the flavors explode in your mouth. Are you seated at a table to eat? Are other people around you? If so, are conversations going on? What do you hear, see, smell, touch, and taste around your favorite meal?

The following longer activity, a sort of imagery aerobics, is designed for a more intensive experience of stimulating imagery. You may want to put this on tape so you can listen to the instructions rather than trying to remember them. Take your time with this activity.

Be seated in a comfortable position in a quiet room. Close your eyes and focus on your breathing. Follow your breath in and out, simply paying attention to each breath.

Do this for a few minutes until you feel centered and focused.

Now imagine you're walking on a path in the woods. It's a clearly marked path; the day is comfortably warm. Feel the soft forest earth beneath your feet as you walk. See the sunlight breaking through the trees. Feel the warm air on your face and arms as you walk. Listen to the birds singing or the rustle of a squirrel as it forages among leaves and then scurries up a tree.

You continue walking through the woods as the path becomes less clearly marked. You feel very relaxed, enjoying your walk. Soon you can barely make out the path. You keep walking, taking in your surroundings, a feeling of contentment moving through you. Now you see you have come to the edge of the woods. Before you lies a beautiful meadow, thick with soft grass and bathed in warm sunlight. You step into the meadow and feel a sense of peacefulness, of calm. Feel the sponge-like grass beneath your feet as you explore this meadow. Smell the sweet, clean air. Listen for birds or other animals. Hear the gentle falling of water over rocks in a stream running through this meadow.

Now as you explore, you discover a picnic basket, and upon opening it, you find some of your favorite foods. Obviously this basket was meant for you, so you help yourself to the food. Sitting on the soft grass, perhaps leaning on a tree or a rock, smelling the fresh air and listening to the gentle waterfall, you bite into this delectable treat. It tastes as wonderful as you expected it to. Continue enjoying your picnic, taking all the time you need.

When you're finished, experience all the sensory

impressions of this place. Know that you can return here anytime you want—to exercise your imagery or simply to relax.

Now begin taking five deep breaths, allowing your awareness to shift to the breaths. Each breath brings you closer to full waking consciousness. With the fifth breath you are fully alert and awake and aware of the room around you.

While this is an excellent activity for stimulating internal imagery and setting up new pathways to creativity, it's also good for relaxation. And creativity occurs under relaxed conditions, not under stress.

Ha-Ha = Aha!

Have you laughed today? If not, maybe it's time to take a laugh break. This can be simple: take a moment to recall something funny that has happened to you, either recently or in the past. An event often becomes humorous when it turns out differently than anticipated. Or think of a joke, a humorous scene from a movie or television show, or maybe a cartoon. What can you do right now that would make you laugh?

Laughter is a remarkable human gift. But have you ever wondered why we laugh? When we experience something as funny, we have made a mental leap from one thought to another. A sudden change in direction, a quick shift from one line of thinking to another makes us laugh. Creativity requires a similar mental leap.

Like any skill, mental agility must be practiced, and humor will help you accomplish this. Laughter exercises the mind by making quick mental shifts and stretches the boundaries of thinking to allow more room for ideas. Too many people approach the creative process as serious business. They want to know the "right" way to become creative.

By contrast, I encourage people to act silly when they are trying to expand their creativity. *Silly* derives from the Greek word *selig*, which means blessed, and the Middle English *seli*, meaning innocent. Creative people often have a childlike innocence in their approach to life and its problems. Being silly, nurturing our sense of humor, and laughing move us closer to a state of blessed innocence, to our creativity.

The key in using humor to stimulate creativity is to make yourself laugh. Children's author Byrd Baylor once told me about a young man she encountered after giving a speech to a college audience. He was upset with Baylor because, in his view, she didn't take her work seriously while he did. "I explained to him that, indeed, I have been serious about my writing since I was eight. But I don't take *myself* seriously." This attitude allows Byrd to continually refine her writing ability while imparting a sense of childlike wonder to her books.

A sense of humor can be encouraged in many ways. Thinking of jokes or funny lines from a movie or television program is an excellent warm-up for the mental flexibility required of creative efforts. Reading a joke book before going into a problem-solving session or prior to starting a task requiring creativity can help set the proper tone. I encourage you to begin your own joke book. For example, I carry index cards with me to jot down humorous thoughts I have during the day or to make a note of funny things that happen to other people. Sometimes I find an unusual story in the newspaper that I find entertaining. I clip it and tape it to a card. The cards are handy for me to write on and to read through if I need a chuckle. I don't care about whether someone else might think something is funny—it's *my* joke book. When I'm feeling stuck and far from my creativity, I have quick access to something that can help me readjust my perspective, to shift into a creative mode.

We have all attended too many meetings where the problem-solving process becomes bogged down with unimaginative solutions, where dullness prevails. During these times, we can enliven the atmosphere with a joke, perhaps one directed at ourselves, and challenge others to do the same. The group can laugh its way out of its lethargy. (Humor directed at another person or at someone's idea isn't advisable.) As we stimulate laughter, combining mental leaps and innocence, imaginative solutions will follow.

Probably all meetings ought to start with telling funny stories or jokes to stimulate the group's creativity. Group members who have difficulty remembering jokes can bring in a cartoon or something from their joke book. If a brainstorming session begins to bog down, reaching for the ridiculous can stretch the limits of the group's thinking.

Laughing makes us lose our inhibitions, at least temporarily. This loosening breaks us out of routine thinking and helps us see an issue from a new perspective. Humor warms up our mental flexibility for making creative leaps. In other words, *ha-ha* leads us to *aha!*

$\mathcal{B}$ecoming More Spontaneous

Creativity thrives on the unplanned and the unexpected. Serendipity, the accident that happens while we're looking for something else, frequently occurs during the creative process. A researcher at 3M spills a chemical on her canvas shoe and discovers Scotchgard.[1] Dance pioneer Mary Wigman expresses her joy to co-workers by clapping her hands together and a new dance is born.[2] Has this ever happened to you? You've been working on something, apparently moving in one direction, when suddenly a whole new idea occurs to you.

Obviously we can't plan randomness, but we can stimulate the likelihood of it happening. And we can set ourselves up for noticing it. One way is relying on our holistic process to pull together as much variety as possible, entertain many possibilities, and combine them into new, sometimes unlikely, outcomes. Another is becoming more spontaneous in all areas of our lives.

The living, dynamic energy of creativity stagnates under the weight of routine. Methodical behaviors lead to predictable thoughts. Being creative means breaking away from the conventional.

But habits are tracked into the old part of the brain, and breaking them requires diligent effort. For example, once we've mastered the bicycle, we'll always be able to ride, regardless of how much time has passed since we last mounted a two-wheeler. We don't have to think of every movement when we drive a car or take a shower or brush our teeth. These routine actions are embedded into our brains. Habits are useful, even necessary, but they can also spawn routine thinking.

Traditional education also trains us out of spontaneity with its emphasis on strict adherence to rules (outline first!) and distrust of anything that can't be measured. Included in the latter category are feelings and innate wisdom, two essential ingredients in our creative process. We can't expect ourselves to suddenly become creatively spontaneous in problem-solving if we rigidly structure other areas of our lives. So, many of us need to break up routines in thinking and behaving.

I'm not suggesting we never plan anything, never make lists, or live our lives in chaos. What I do want to encourage is relaxing routine. We can teach ourselves it's OK to bypass the old part of our brain with its desire for sameness that inhibits creative thinking. We're striving for a small change at first, nothing so dramatic that it becomes frightening in its newness. To gain a sense of the feeling that accompanies breaking up habits, try this simple activity:

> Clasp your hands and fingers together. Notice which thumb is on top. Now open your hands, shift your fingers so that the other thumb is on top and clasp them together again. How does this new arrangement feel?

Most people describe a "funny" or "uncomfortable" sensation. The shift doesn't elicit strong feelings of discomfort, but it brings on a mild sense that something is different. This is the feeling we're working for as we break routines. When you're stuck in a set way of thinking that's inhibiting your creativity, see what you can do to elicit a feeling of "the wrong thumb's on top." You might try some of the following suggestions:

Look for places where you can disrupt habits. If you usually eat breakfast before you shower, reverse the order. Alter your bathing routine. If you shower from the top down, start from the bottom and work your way up. Or wash the right arm, the left leg, your neck, left arm, back, right leg, trunk, face, and hair. Vary the order every shower.

Use a different route to and from work. Try side streets. Shake yourself out of seeing/not seeing the same things every day.

At regularly scheduled meetings, we tend to sit in the same location. This place orientation arises from the old brain we're overriding to be more creative. Sitting in a different place each meeting will help accomplish this bypass. You'll displace someone else when you choose a new seat, but you can assure yourself and others this disruption is healthy for everyone's creativity!

Keep looking for ways you can alter your routine. Vary the time you take lunch. Rearrange your office furniture or things on your desk. Work from the other side or from one end of your desk. Or if you're really feeling stuck, move to another part of your office or to a different room.

Away from your workplace, you can continue having fun with the challenge of becoming more spontaneous. Take an unplanned walk around your neighborhood. Drive with no particular destination in mind, exploring areas of your city or countryside you've seldom traveled. (It's a good idea to have an updated map with you—just in case.)

Try doing things "on the spur of the moment," especially if you're the type of person who usually plans the day's activities ahead of time. Go to a restaurant you've never tried. Attend a concert of music new to your ears. Devote one day a week to being spontaneous.

By disrupting our routines and breaking habituated behavior patterns, we teach ourselves to be comfortable with newness. We're learning how to bypass the old brain that can keep us trapped in dull, routine thinking. The more spontaneity we bring into our lives, the more creative we'll be.

Making the Ordinary Extraordinary

A client once lamented that her intensive art-school education permanently altered the way she observes everything. She can't look out her studio window and see a simple desert scene. The sky, earth, cactus, rocks, and occasional bird or lizard are nuances of lighting, color, perspective, and line. "Seeing like this is both a curse and a blessing," she said. But an intensely vivid way of seeing is necessary for an artist.

Most of us never develop an artist's eye, but living creatively challenges us to develop our ability to view the ordinary in extraordinary ways. This search isn't for new landscapes, it's for seeing the same landscapes differently.

Many activities in this book shake up your usual vision. For example, in the previous chapter, "Becoming More Spontaneous," you were encouraged to break up routines. Driving to and from work using alternate routes accomplishes this goal and stimulates you to see things you don't ordinarily see. Sitting in a different place in a meeting provides a novel view of the meeting.

Creative insight results from perceiving the usual in unusual ways. Children accomplish this naturally. A spoon is always much more than a mere eating utensil to them. It's a tool for cultivating the earth, a tongue depressor, a musical instrument. The possibilities are endless. The original purpose for the spoon must be discarded so new uses can be explored. As long as we see the spoon merely as something used for eating, we can't conceive of other possibilities. Our creative imagination is stymied by our preconceived ideas.

Hence, Jean Houston's first law: "Concept louses up percept."[1] In other words, how we conceptualize a problem, task, or any challenge will determine how we perceive it. And our perception will guide our attempts to resolve the issue. If we fail to involve our creativity in the concept stage, we'll be unable to arrive at a creative resolution. Shaking up how we see something in the initial step engages our creativity.

The following activity is designed to encourage you to suspend your beliefs about a common object and reconceptualize its possible uses. This is more effective when it is done with several people so everyone can play off each other's ideas. Give yourself at least a half hour of undisturbed time with this activity. Before you begin, have a rubber band nearby.

Close your eyes and focus on your breathing. Bring your attention to each breath as you inhale and exhale. Do this for several minutes until you feel relaxed and centered.

Now imagine you are living on a planet in another solar system—a planet whose inhabitants explore other galaxies. You are an anthropologist getting ready to visit a newly discovered world. Your task is to learn as much as you can about its culture, mores, religion, political and economic systems, and current state of technology.

You enter your spacecraft along with other members of the exploration team. You settle into a comfortable chair for the short flight. Through the windows of your spacecraft you see other planets and stars along your journey.

Soon you near your destination—a blue planet, the third from its sun in this solar system, called Earth by its inhabitants. Your spaceship lands at a preselected site and you are guided into a room in an earthling building. Here you are given an object discovered by earlier explorers and believed vital to the entire planet. From this one object you and the other anthropologists are expected to determine as much as you can about Earth and its inhabitants.

Now open your eyes and, using the rubber band as the object, make assumptions about Earth and its population in as many aspects as you can. Ask yourself what uses this object might have. What do these functions tell you about Earth beings? What could this object symbolize? What does it represent with regard to religion, culture, economics, technology, or politics?

Any suggestion regarding the rubber band is acceptable as long as it doesn't reflect the "real" use. The more outrageous, the better. Continue with the activity as long as you can, playfully pushing the boundaries of your imagination.

When you've finished generating as many possibilities as you can, put the rubber band near the place where you do most of your creative work. The next time you find yourself having difficulty creatively conceptualizing a problem or task, pick up the rubber band and allow it to return you to the mindset of an anthropologist from a distant planet with no preconceived ideas. Suspend your beliefs and stimulate your creative process.

The imagery part of this activity, seeing yourself as an anthropologist from another world and traveling through space to Earth, helps alter your belief system. Simply picking up the rubber band and speculating as to its possible uses is difficult without first doing something to change how you're seeing.

As you practice/play with suspending your beliefs, you'll be able to switch off the old and begin exploring new possibilities. Common objects make entertaining targets. A shower becomes a sacred ritual designed to re-establish a connection between the individual and the forces of nature, in this case, rain. An overhead projector becomes a powerful instrument—so intense it can't be used alone, only in groups—that teaches humans how to be humble by making insignificant information larger and more important.

Learning to see the ordinary in extraordinary ways takes practice. Sometimes asking questions helps: I know the common ideas I have about this issue. If I put those aside, what might I think about it? What other uses or possibilities might exist for this problem? If I didn't know what I know, what would I believe?

By suspending our beliefs and teaching ourselves to have an artist's vision when we look at challenges, we learn to see in uncommon ways. We abandon our narrow conceptions and tap into creative resources.

Preventing Burnout

The Price of Stress

We've all heard how stress ravages us physically and emotionally. Many of us have tried relaxation, visualization, and biofeedback to de-stress ourselves, while others have changed jobs or careers, or moved to another part of the country. These efforts result in varying levels of success. Living a relatively stress-free life would make most of us healthier, happier, and more receptive to our creativity. But stress accumulated over a period of time has serious implications.

Prolonged stress causes burnout, an often-misused phrase describing everything from being tired to overly tense to having our energy seriously depleted. When we can take some time off work to relax, then return feeling renewed, we've been suffering from fatigue which may have many causes. Our diet may not be providing proper nutrition; we may be lacking sleep; we may have upset our internal clock from extensive travel or working different shifts. In any case, we recover and go back to our work, so we haven't burned out. If the trigger for our stress is inherent in our job, our recovery will be temporary.

True burnout happens by tapping into and draining off our sustaining life-force energy. Once this occurs, we may never be able to repair the damage. When we force ourselves into someone else's idea of who and what we should be, denying our true selves and failing to mature into a self-defined individual, we set ourselves up for a life of extreme stress and potential burnout.

I once received an urgent phone call from a client who had pushed herself to the edge of burning out. A few hours later Becky was sobbing in my office, explaining she had allowed herself to become too stressed by her work. She held a position she had worked for and been promoted into about a year previously. She was exceptionally competent and her boss continually asked more of her. Although she told him repeatedly she couldn't handle additional responsibilities, he kept giving her more tasks, many belonging to a less-competent peer.

My client's situation was similar to what many women experience in the workplace. Historically our domain has been the home, where we have been in charge of everything. Thus, we are enculturated to believe we're responsible for every task needing to be accomplished. We carry this attitude into our careers, believing we can and should do it all. Becky fulfilled this expectation when she negated her own protests about being required to do too much by always saying yes to her boss's requests. She realized the full impact her situation was having on her only after she enjoyed a relaxing vacation. While this may sound contradictory, it's fairly common.

Reason might tell us that after a week of complete rest, she ought to have been better able to handle the stress. In fact, this reprieve enabled her to fully experience the damage being done to her by her work and the situation she was in. The contrast between feeling like herself and dealing with a noxious situation became too great. The fifth day she was back at her desk, she called for help. After three more weeks away from her job and some intensive therapy, she had several critical realizations.

First, she had a driving need to prove herself exceptionally competent. Hence, she was unable to make her boss hear her protests about excessive workloads. Second, feeling as if she should handle everything, she allowed no room for cutting back on or delegating projects when new ones were added. Finally, Becky accepted herself as an exceptionally creative individual who needed a constant outlet for her creativity. Ironically, her job had provided more means for creative expression when she began. The more responsibilities her boss added, the less time she had for the creative aspects, considered less important and delegated to an assistant.

Ultimately, her inability to express her creative self led to her near-burnout. I describe her situation as near-burnout because after a year and a half of working in fields where she could express herself creatively, Becky was recovered. In cases of true burnout, the individual may never fully recuperate. The drain on that person's energy leaves her with no resources for changing. She's just too tired. But the exhaustion goes on and on. With no energy, she lacks motivation and enthusiasm. She may even distrust her ability to make decisions. After all, she made the choices that resulted in the burnout! She is paralyzed. Working through such an event requires the help of a professional and usually takes a long time.

I remember a student who revealed that five years previously she had suffered a mental breakdown. She left her career and went under a psychiatrist's care. Since that time, she had been unwilling to trust herself. She had extreme difficulty making decisions, in some cases avoiding them for several years. Some exploration into her background revealed that, like so many others who have burned out, this young woman was engaged in work unsuited to her. In this case, her parents chose her career for her. She felt burdened by other family obligations, leaving her no time to explore and experience her unique wants and needs.

When we engage in work that isn't ours—the teacher who is really a writer, the accountant who is really a therapist, the housewife who is really an architect, the minister who is really a corporate executive—we set ourselves up for critically depleting our energy. Anger, rage, and depression can all be symptoms of impending burnout, just as they can be indicators that we are failing to give expression to our creative selves.

In earlier sections in this book we explored some of the negative ways repressed creativity expresses itself: depression, anger, alcoholism, indecisiveness, low self-esteem. At the very least, stifled creativity leads to stress which can cause burnout. This serious situation can be avoided by making certain we are giving expression to our inherent creative abilities.

The Antidote to Stress

When I ask women about their experiences with burnout and what they do to prevent it, I get very similar responses. Women frequently say that doing too many things at one time, spreading themselves too thin, and paying too much attention to business, to planning and organizing, take away from their creative energy. A commonly suggested solution is to devote more time to relaxation and balance. Dancer Mary Ann Brehm states, "I try to pay attention to pacing activities and keeping myself in tune with my needs for a balance of activity and rest and time for integrating, that is, cogitating about savoring, taking credit for creative activities and accomplishments before piling on the next." In a similar vein, Andrea Gold, president of a speakers' bureau, says she needs to "do everything in moderation—balance physical, mental, emotional, spiritual."

Being creative in all areas of our lives contributes to our health and opens us to becoming a constant channel of creative energy. This way, excessive stress can't build up. Chores become projects stimulating to our creative expression. Routine tasks give us time for speculating about varieties of ways to solve more complex issues. We naturally gravitate toward jobs and careers requiring our strengths and allowing creative expression. We're not going to burn out under these circumstances.

When clients experience the flow of creative energy through them, infusing it into all aspects of their lives, they often describe themselves as feeling physically lighter. Positive energy pushes away the negativity which bombards us all day long, contributing to stress, illness, and a lack of enthusiasm for life. Reading or watching the news is a primary source of negativity. Driving in congested traffic frequently stimulates the passage of negativity from one driver to another. Unhappy, depressed, and angry people can dump their negative energy onto us and we can unwittingly take it on as our own. Our stress goes up, we move closer to burning out and further away from being creative. We may pass some of our bad feelings on to others by snapping at co-workers, becoming impatient with our children, or yelling at loved ones. Staying with a flow of creative energy breaks this cycle. Over and over, women tell me that their creativity gets stifled by two major factors: stress and exposure to negative, critical people. So keeping negativity away from us and cleaned out of our bodies is important.

Like any other change in behavior, becoming a channel for positive, creative energy takes practice. This simple clearing technique can help clean out any negativity we've accumulated in ourselves and keep us from taking on more.

You can do this activity sitting or standing, but don't try it lying down. Your feet need to be on the floor.

Close your eyes and imagine white light or clear water coming in through the bottoms of your feet and moving up the front of your body. Imagine as it moves it takes with it any negativity or stress and leaves a feeling of relaxation. When the light/water reaches the top of your head, let it flow down the back of your head, through your shoulders and back, all the way down to the bottoms of your feet. Feel it taking negativity and stress as it moves. Release the negativity out the bottoms of your feet and imagine it is being cleansed by the light/water.

Coordinating this activity with your breathing can make it easier. As you inhale, you're pulling the light/water in and up the front of your body. As you exhale, the light/water moves down the back of your body and you release negativity to be cleansed.

Complete this cycle as many times as you need to feel relaxed and relieved of stress. If you practice this simple technique under calm conditions, you can use it to quickly clear yourself whenever you begin feeling tense. Now take it one step further.

Once you're free of tension, you can call upon creative energy to come into your body. You may image it coming in through the bottoms of your feet or through the top of your head. Whichever source seems right to you, use it. You may also see a color associated with your creative energy, sense a texture, or hear a sound. Use any image to make the experience more vivid. Allow the creative energy to flow through your body, from your feet to your hands, and through your head.

Now you can direct this energy to any part of your body. If you're working on problem-solving, you can direct your creative energy to your head. If you're trying to be more innovative about relationships, direct it to your heart. If you're painting or sculpting, channel the energy into your hands. Once you've established this directed flow of creative energy, you are ready to begin working/playing.

You won't absorb any negativity that comes along when you are already filled with creative energy. And you'll be much less likely to bring on your own stress or negative energy with a flow of creativity moving through you. Creative action occurs when we're relaxed and open to creative energy.

Living a creative lifestyle where we apply our strengths in innovative ways to all aspects of our lives means we are living healthily.

Loving Your Creative Self

What's the ideal relationship? It may have ingredients like shared compassion, caring, nurturing, love, fun, passion. We want to be heard and we want our partner to talk to us about intimate feelings and concerns. A balance of independence and dependence would be healthy, so we can be supported for who we are while feeling we have someone to depend on. An even exchange of give and take, of nurturing and being nurtured happens in this relationship. While it would take time and effort to develop, the rewards would be returned exponentially.

This book is devoted to helping you develop an ideal relationship with your creativity.

Creativity exists to make our lives better, more fun, and interesting. It provides us with tools for meeting challenges and coping with adversity while giving us an outlet for a unique aspect of ourselves. But we can't just throw some inner switch and expect the creativity to gush forth. We need to develop a rapport with our creativity, nurturing our relationship with our creative self the way we would any other important partnership.

We need to know what stimulates our creativity and what we can do to facilitate the process. We need to understand it at an intimate level. If we cling to mystical notions about creativity or the idea that it is reserved for the gifted few, we can't be close to our creative self. No one can develop intimacy with someone shrouded in mystery or elevated to a pedestal. Interacting with our creative aspect is encountering a healthy, vibrant part of us. It can become one of the most important relationships in our lives. This interaction carries with it all the passion, excitement, fear, disappointment, and rewards of any other union. And its development can follow the same path.

Adapting Susan Campbell's five-stage model for relationships as described in *The Couple's Journey: Intimacy as a Path to Wholeness* can give us a framework for developing a rapport with our creativity.[1] It can guide us in progressing to a deep relationship with our creative self. You will probably recognize many of the characteristics of each phase.

Romance

In the first stage, romance, we become enthralled with the idea of making great art or writing best-sellers or being responsible for a revolutionary technological advance. We're in love with our creativity. We can be caught in the illusion that simply by wanting to be more creative, we will be. Especially important in this first stage is the enthusiasm generated by our initial attraction to the idea of doing creative work or of becoming more creative in our lives. This excitement can carry us through many challenges to developing a balanced union with the creative self.

Being in love with our creativity awakens us to our own possibilities. It opens us to the sheer joy of creating and connects us to our passions. ◄ With this enthusiasm we can plunge ahead confidently. Unfortunately, many of these feelings can fade as we encounter "reality."

See
Where's the Passion?
p. 105

Power Struggle

The second stage presents the greatest difficulty: the power struggle. After the romance wears off and the hard work begins, we can find ourselves struggling to force our creative process and the end results into a preconceived mold. Meanwhile, the process strives to express itself its way. We end up in conflict. Rather than encouraging our creative self to communicate naturally, we may attempt to follow what we think is the "correct" process or to validate only tangible products, leaving much of our work unrecognized. Not only will we fail to give expression to our true creative nature, but we'll also resent our creativity for not meeting our expectations. Have you ever found yourself in this type of dilemma?

Our task in resolving this inner conflict lies with recognizing and honoring the distinctive process and products our creativity has to offer. Learning to trust the process and accepting that our creativity exists for our well-being are critical. At the same time we take care of our needs, balancing creative work with other aspects of our lives. We give up trying to force our creativity into preconceived ideas while our creative self learns how to work with us. We may have to give up our illusions about becoming a best-selling novelist as we uncover a genius for teaching, for example. We discover in this power struggle who we are as unique beings and learn how expressing our creative gifts can support our individuality. We make peace with our creative self, joining in full partnership with it.

Stability

The next phase is stability, where, by accepting who we are as creative individuals and how our unique creativity manifests, we can welcome change. It's part of the paradox of creativity that it is nurtured in an atmosphere of security from which we can take risks and invite the change accompanying creative expression. The more intimate we are with our unique process, the better understanding we have of what it needs. One time it may be stimulated by the discipline of working on a project for several hours while another time it may need to retreat into our less-conscious awareness as we engage in some unrelated activity such as physical exercise or watching a movie.

We're devoted in this third stage to nurturing our creativity and ourselves even when it means facing some inner conflict and seeing it through to a constructive resolution. While many blocks in the creative process occur at the power-struggle stage, the resolution to those blocks occurs in the stability phase. Standing on this kind of solid ground, we can move forward.

Commitment

Commitment, the fourth stage in our evolving relationship, is typified by a feeling of being able to be who we truly are as we express our unique self. We've stopped trying to force conformity on ourselves or our creativity and have accepted change as a constant. With a solid trust in our creative aspect, we rely on creativity to improve the quality of our lives. As we increasingly give expression to this unique part of ourselves and begin living a creative lifestyle, we discover that this expression influences those around us to be more creative.

This level of commitment to ourselves as creative beings means we fully engage in life, taking responsibility for our successes and learning from mistakes, always involved in the experience. As we move through this phase, we continually find ways to express ourselves creatively.

Co-Creation

In the fifth stage, co-creation, we synthesize all the lessons we've learned from the previous phases. We understand we have multiple options for how we relate and respond to events in our lives; we create our experience. From this perspective, we may decide to carry our innovations into the world. Women actively engaged in making creative works commonly talk about wanting to give something beautiful to the world. These women are living this final stage in the relationship journey and are consciously contributing to human evolution through their creative works. These aren't true believers out to change the world to their mold. They are the women who accept that the world may reject their works because these expressions are at odds with the status quo. At the same time they understand that for them to be fully human, they must share with others who they uniquely are.

Communicating with Your Creative Self

Virtually every activity in this book is designed to enhance your relationship with your creativity. Dialoguing techniques are especially useful for opening communication and increasing understanding between you and your creative self. We've explored other written dialogues in this book. The intent of the following activity is to nurture the beginning of a long-term, committed relationship. In starting the dialogue, remember to begin with an open-ended question and avoid asking why.

Your dialogue might start like this:

Me: What can I do to use you more in my everyday life?

Creative Self: Acknowledge me when I do something.

Me: How can I do that?

C.S.: Just say, "That was a very creative idea you had, Diane."

Me: That sounds too simple.

C.S.: Don't complicate things. Acknowledging is simple.

Put this book aside for now and have a conversation

with your creative self. Open up the communication to continue the journey you are taking.

Give the dialogue time to flow so you feel as if you're not working to deliberately construct questions or responses.

This might take ten or fifteen minutes or more. There may also be times when the dialogue flows easier than at other times. The more often you give yourself the opportunity to talk with and listen to your creative self, the more you will find your creativity available to you. You can tell your creativity what you want from it and ask what it wants from you. This technique can be used in any phase of your relationship.

Building a positive alliance with the creative self takes time, effort, and patience, just as developing any intimacy does. Because creativity makes our lives better, every effort invested in improving that rapport brings multiple benefits. Eventually, our lives will seem less split into the creative and the routine and more of our experiences will be dominated by the former. Then we'll feel more like a whole person living creatively.

$\mathcal{L}$etting Your Dreams
Create for You

Sometimes they're mysterious, sometimes frightening. But don't worry, it's *only* a dream. We have varied reactions to the world that comes to us while we sleep. Psychoanalysts Sigmund Freud and Carl Jung spent much of their professional lives attempting to make sense out of their patients' sleeping realities. Books and workshops on the subject abound, each promising to help us unlock the meanings hidden in our dreams, enabling us to use them to enhance our lives. What kind of relationship do you have with your dreams?

In spite of a pervasive interest in dreams, misconceptions flourish. And we need to understand some fundamentals about the dream world before using it to augment our creativity.

The Reality of Dreams

First, everyone dreams. Some people may have difficulty remembering their dreams, but this can be overcome. Often, when people say they can't recall dreams, their last memory is of a nightmare.[1] They've been scared out of wanting to remember. This fear can be dealt with by realizing that dreams often convey messages which are helpful in our lives. Sometimes when we don't attend to them, dreams will go to extremes—even frightening ones—to get our attention.

We may also have trouble remembering dreams because they don't carry the charge necessary to implant them into the brain's memory.[2] We remember an event because an electrical and chemical change takes place in the brain. Our waking experiences can activate this memory process more easily than our dreams. So we have to put an electrical charge onto our dreams, as the activities throughout this section are designed to do.

Second, no one can tell us what our dreams mean. I cringe when someone says, "My therapist told me my dream meant . . . ." or "This dream book translates my dreams for me." The language of dreams is imagery, composed of symbols which may have several interpretations. All our life experiences, from religious beliefs to the literature we read and the movies we watch, influence our personal imagery. In addition, we're exposed to cultural and universal imagery as well. We can use help in sorting out all this, but ultimately, *we* decide what our dreams are trying to tell us.

Finally, while some people invest much time and effort into understanding their dream imagery, others dismiss dreams as if they were meaningless or even useless. When I check my computer thesaurus, it tells me the opposite of *dream* is *reality*. Our language encourages us to believe that dreams aren't real, that they contain no truth. But dreams are as real an experience as any event in our waking life. Anyone who has ever awakened with heart racing from a nightmare or with a physical discomfort exactly like the one they felt in a dream can attest to their tangibility. Besides, knowing what a powerful and complex organ the human brain is, the notion that it would spend any of its effort on something pointless is absurd.

Understanding Our Dreams Our Way

So the best place to begin building a relationship with our dream world is by discarding any misconceptions we've held. Our dreams exist to assist us in making our lives better. Through their symbolic language, they give us information about ourselves we would have difficulty gaining any other way. Dreams are an important part of the psyche that can enhance all other aspects of our lives, especially creativity.

Many techniques designed for understanding dreams are archaeological, that is, they encourage traveling into the dream world and digging around, sometimes even forcing meaning out of the images. Some approaches suggest doing physical harm to, even killing, frightening images. This is supposed to make us feel stronger. But our dream images arise from our psyche—they're part of us. So I'm opposed to any violent tactics applied to dream symbolism. These methods break down communication, they don't facilitate it.

Rather than the archaeological view, I prefer to relate to the dream reality from an anthropological perspective. This means we're trying to understand another culture, one with its own language. With this attitude we're encouraged to respect our dream world just as we would any other society we're trying to understand.

The language of this internal culture is imagery. As we discussed earlier, we can have three layers of meaning to our symbolism: personal, cultural, and universal. Some excellent books have been written describing these latter two types. Anyone serious about communicating with the dream world ought to invest in one. These aren't books that tell you what a particular image means as if only one possibility existed; instead, they present a variety of interpretations. For example, the book I use devotes about one and a half columns to discussing the symbolism of a bee as found in many cultures throughout the world.[3]

But if I want to know what a bee symbolizes, I don't go to my imagery book first. I need to try understanding it from a personal perspective. One of the best ways to do this is to dialogue with the image, the same way we've talked with various aspects of our creative selves in other activities in this book. Avoiding the question, "Why are you in my dream?" which will only result in rambling vagaries, we can begin by asking what purpose the image or symbol serves in the dream or what it represents. My written dialogue might look like this:

Me: Bee, what are you telling me in the dream?
Bee: Busy, busy, busy. You're busy as a bee.
Me: That's really trite.
Bee: Trite but true. You need to slow down.

When the writing seems to flow automatically, we know we're in rapport with the image. Once I grasp an image, my understanding of the entire dream is enhanced.

Or the dialogue can happen face-to-face. By vividly recalling the dream, you can talk directly with any part of the dream at any point in the dream. This activity is very much like daydreaming.

Be seated in a comfortable position. Focus your attention on your breathing, relaxing more with each breath.

Now begin recalling your dream. See it as you did the first time. When you encounter the thing you want to talk to, simply stop the dream and focus on it. Engage it in conversation, asking questions that will help you to understand this symbol. It doesn't matter that it might be something that usually doesn't talk, like a wall or a bee. This symbol is in your dream for a reason: to give you a message. By talking with it you are opening yourself to deeper understanding.

When you feel as if the dialogue is finished, thank the symbol for talking with you. Refocus your attention on your breathing and let yourself come back to the room.

If my dialogue runs its course and I still don't feel as if I've gotten to the image's meaning, then I consult my symbol book. Many possible interpretations may exist for the image, so I pay careful attention to how I react as I read the list of possibilities. One usually stands out over the others; it just feels right.

To overcome an inability to remember dreams, we need to pay attention to them. We can affirm as we're falling asleep, "I will remember my dreams when I awaken." Repeat this statement several times while falling asleep. By keeping a dream journal beside the bed and writing in it immediately upon awakening, we reinforce our desire to communicate with our dreams. Writing anything we recall from the dream world is important, even if it's only a vague feeling. Sometimes one or two lines can stimulate us to remember more. By writing the dream in first person, present tense, we call up the vividness of the experience. An entry might sound like this:

> I am in my office, sitting at my desk. I get the feeling I'm the only person here. I don't see or sense any co-workers. A bee starts buzzing around my head. At first I feel threatened. . . .

Noting feelings throughout the narration is important to understanding the total impact of the dream. Over a period of time a dream journal can reflect our personal growth, new insights into our behavior, and sometimes even foretell future events.

After developing a strong rapport with their dreams, some people begin to engage in lucid dreaming, where we realize we're dreaming in the midst of it. In other words, I may be dreaming that I'm in my office and being pestered by a bee while, at the same time, I know I'm dreaming. With this awareness, we can orchestrate what's happening in the dream, taking charge of the events and outcome.

Having Our Dreams Work for Us

While these facets to our relationship with the dream world are fascinating and helpful, our dreams can be enormously helpful to our creativity. Have you ever had the solution to a problem present itself or seen a completed painting while you're asleep? This usually happens after we've been working on a project, trying to solve a problem, sketching the painting, or outlining the plot and characters for a novel. But the resolution can come to us unexpectedly. We don't know when we're going to be presented with this help. An artist-client tells me she sketches paintings before putting them onto canvas, but when she sees the completed work in a dream, she knows how she will use color in the piece. While her dream version doesn't have all the detail of the finished work, she has enough information to begin painting the canvas. Many of us have had similar experiences of working on a problem—it often seems to involve math—to the point of giving up. Then, as we sleep, the answer is presented to us.

A journalist tells me, "Since childhood, I have thought about creative problems as I was going to sleep. I would wake up with solutions, or ideas that at least chipped away at obstacles." When I asked Andrea, a business owner, what nurtured her creativity, she replied that sleeping on a problem "plants seeds to a higher source." A university professor told me that dreams stimulate her creative process, and then she added, "I have great dreams."

The logical, rational part of our brains isn't very creative. Bypassing it in order to have access to our creative aspect is sometimes tricky, as we've observed in other parts of this book. But while we're sleeping, our logical processes are muted, allowing more creative ones to dominate. To take full advantage of this, we have to be doing our homework: researching the problem, making the sketches, writing notes about plot and characterization. Then this information can combine with our creative resources, using the dream as the medium.

While I was working on my doctoral dissertation, I struggled with a model for women's creativity. I knew the dominant, four-step linear model didn't represent women's experience of this wonderful process. But even after several weeks of searching, I couldn't come up with an appropriate model. Finally, the answer came to me during a dream in which a goddess directed my attention to a flattened spiral. She reached into the center and pulled it out, somewhat like a slinky. No words were exchanged, but when I awoke, I knew I had been presented with the spiral as a model for women's creative process. The more I worked with the spiral, the more sense it made. While the image was presented to me in a dream, I had to work out the applications.

Working with Your Dreams

Yes, our dreams can be pathways to our creative selves. But we have to prime the pumps first, then put the answer into tangible form. Our dream world can be helpful, but it can't do all our work for us.

The assistance our dreams can give us doesn't have to arrive haphazardly. By communicating with the dream reality, we can orchestrate its responses to our needs. Rather than trying to discover the meaning of a dream, we put our efforts into building a rapport with our dream world. As with the activities discussed earlier, we need to relate to our dreams through the language of imagery. Instead of waiting for our dreams to come up with an image and then trying to figure out what it means, we can suggest to our dream reality that it use particular images to represent certain things. The color red, for instance, might mean we're on the wrong track in problem-solving, while green might mean our work is correct. We can negotiate for these symbols through written dialogue with the dream world or by talking to it directly. The latter approach works best when we're in an altered state, as during meditation or while falling asleep or waking up.

In other words, we can talk directly to our dream world, specifically asking that certain images represent aspects of our lives. A written dialogue might look like this:

Me: Dream world, I need your help.

D.W.: What's up?

Me: Sometimes I'm not sure I'm on the right track. You know, making the right decision or working on a problem the best way.

D.W.: So what can I do?

Me: Let's develop a way of communicating. I trust your wisdom about these things, so when I ask for your help in solving a problem, if you show me the color red I'll know I'm going in the wrong direction. Green means I'm OK.

D.W.: I can do that. Red = wrong. Green = OK.

Me: Right. Thanks.

Getting a strong visual image of the red and green helps. Or you might want to have the same conversation in your head instead of in writing. With this arrangement, you can ask your dream world to assist you. As you're falling asleep, simply review the problem you're trying to solve and ask your dream world for help. It can then let you know, using colors or other symbols you recognize, how you are doing with the problem.

We can also ask for assistance with a particular problem in other ways. While we're in the twilight zone between being awake and asleep, we can review the issue and ask the dream world for a solution. Or we can request help with writing or creating some work. At the same time, we should give ourselves the suggestion that, when we awaken, we will remember our dreams. Then follow the ideas described earlier for writing in a dream journal. We don't need to wait around for our dream reality to respond to our creative needs. We can ask for what we want when we need it.

I used this approach extensively while writing a science-fiction novel. I would ask my dream world to provide me with the story every evening. In the morning I began writing, usually with only the sensation that my dreams had responded to my request. I seldom knew consciously what I was going to write before I wrote it. After lunch, I napped, again asking for more of the story, enough to last the rest of the writing day. As I did in the morning, I woke up knowing I had the necessary information, but I didn't know the specifics until I was actually writing.

Setting up a communication system of imagery with the dream world enhances our ability to use it creatively. Or it may be enough for some of us to pay attention to our dreams, keep a journal, and ask for assistance when needed. As we develop an interest in our dreams, they'll develop an interest in us, enriching our lives and helping us be more creative.

Nurturing Your Talent

"You've got so much potential! You're just loaded with talent. Why don't you do something with it?" Sound familiar? While the intent of these comments may be positive, the effect can be just the opposite. A great potential, whatever that really is, can become a great burden, especially if we don't believe we're giving expression to our natural abilities. With no outlet for expression, undeveloped talent might just as well not exist.

We may have a gift for art, but only by learning techniques of rendering oil onto canvas, studying perspective, lighting, and color, and continually refining these skills will we develop the ability to become a fine painter. Writers must know a great deal about the structure of language as well as how to create interesting characters and stimulate the reader's imagination, evoking responses to words on paper. Bringing out the natural manager in someone requires learning how to address various work styles through different motivation techniques, orchestrating group energy so people will work together as a cohesive unit, and addressing difficult issues as they arise. Regardless of our innate talents, we need to cultivate the skills of expression along with our creativity to be able to give life to these gifts.

Ideally, nurturing our talents began in childhood. While some of us were fortunate to have had parents who provided the instruction necessary for bringing out our talents, others weren't so lucky. Many parents lacked the money for lessons. Or quality instruction couldn't be found; some teachers did more to stifle and distort talent than to nurture and develop it. Unfortunately, accomplished creative individuals in any field rarely received sufficient education in school to fully develop a talent.

And talent alone isn't enough. Neither are passion, discipline, or creativity by themselves. In addition to these attributes, we need to know how to express ourselves. We've got to acquire skills.

Talent unnurtured at an early age may be difficult to cultivate in adulthood. I've even heard some "experts" claim that gifts neglected in childhood are dead and can't be brought out in the adult. I disagree with this position. Granted, we may never express the talent as fully as we might have from more years of working with it. But as a mature adult, we can bring a clarity and purpose to our creative expressions rarely found even among young "gifted" adults. We can also nurture our creativity along with the skills we learn, giving depth to our natural abilities.

Using Unique Processes to Develop Skills

As we pursue developing our skill level, we must also encourage the expression of our unique creative nature. Tragedy occurs when we attempt to duplicate men's process, as we're frequently tempted to do. The linear model that is prevalent among men dominates as *the* acceptable way to create or think. ◄ It's the process we frequently hear about while we're learning skills. "Do it this way" carries the message that only one means exists for accomplishing an effect. So we conclude we need to imitate the linear. Although copying technique can be an effective way to learn skills, duplicating someone else's process for expressing the talent can be devastating to that gift.

See
In the Beginning . . .
p.3

Ironically, extensive formal education and training in a field increases the likelihood of our imitating a process unnatural to us. I frequently devote many sessions with clients to unlearning the "right" way to create. Shirley represents a typical case. A talented artist, Shirley began art lessons at an early age, culminating with a master's degree in fine arts. She taught college art classes for many years, often the only woman in the department. When she discussed making art with her male colleagues, she heard them agreeing about their process and assumed they were using the "right" method. As Shirley explained, "The men talked about how they made art and all seemed to agree they did it the same way. Their process was very methodical. Since this was all I knew about, I figured I'd better use the same process. Now I realize I have no idea how I create . . . or what my process is."

Although technically Shirley's art is very good, to my eye it is devoid of the feelings usually found in women's art. ◀ Shirley's primary task is allowing her innate process to emerge while eliminating her adopted, unnatural methods.

See
Be Prepared for Provoking a Response
p. 57

Making Mistakes Is OK

Another area requiring caution as we learn skills lies with the expectations we may have of our performance. Most children think nothing of the errors they make while learning. If we hadn't been willing to make mistakes, we would still be crawling! But as adults, we've had many years of developing expertise in a field. When we try something new, we may impose unreasonably high expectations on our abilities, based on our performance in other areas. We expect we'll be just as good at something we're learning as something we've spent many years perfecting. We have to be willing to repeatedly take the risk of making mistakes, working at less than our desired level of expertise while we're learning.

See
**Quieting the
Inner Critic**
p. 229

As we acquire the skills we want, giving ourselves permission to make mistakes, we encourage a natural flow of creativity to merge with our new skills. Our challenge is allowing ourselves to sometimes bumble, sometimes glide our way toward new learning without stopping the process by expecting immediate, wonderful results. (This is discussed at length in "Quieting the Inner Critic.") ▶ Throughout this learning process, we ought to be focusing on our progress, on what we have learned, not on what we haven't, and on the excitement of bringing to life a long-dormant talent.

We can motivate ourselves with rewards: flowers, dinner at a special restaurant, a new blouse, anything that celebrates our progress. Sometimes having a point of comparison is helpful so we can appreciate our skill development. Keeping a journal of activities, reading samples of past work, or listening to tapes of ourselves can provide us with a long-term perspective of our improvement. Having an achievable level of competence as our goal can also contribute to feeling satisfied with our new accomplishments.

Your Talent Doesn't Have to Be Your Profession

I find many adults expect that if they develop the natural gifts they had as a child, then they have to begin earning a living from that talent. I'll let you in on a secret: your innate abilities can be nurtured for pleasure and pleasure only! You may pursue an interest in music just to enjoy singing in the car or the shower. Or you may learn to play an instrument to set your poetry to music, not with the intent of becoming a famous composer, but for the joy of providing a voice for your creative talents.

Once you've decided to learn the skills for expressing your talents, you need to choose how you're going to accomplish your goal. Formal college classes might be appropriate, although noncredit or private instruction might work better. Trying different environments will help you discover the one in which you learn best.

This book is devoted to guiding each of us to fulfilling more of our creative possibilities. While this goal means something different for everyone, we need to build a bridge between our natural talents and our creativity. That bridge is *skill development*. By continually refining our skills while opening channels to our creativity, we give ourselves the opportunity to fully express our innate abilities. Freeing the energy tied up in unused talents can give us more enthusiasm for creative expression in other areas of our lives, for reducing stress, and for gaining more pleasure from life.

Is It Quicksand or a Rock?

Creativity is difficult to study—it's too subjective. If we rely on a creativity test, all we'll know from the results is whether or not a person tests as creative. We won't learn if she or he *expresses* creativity in everyday living. We can talk with creative people, listening to their descriptions of the process, but as soon as the creative experience is verbalized, its essence is gone. Such is the nature of the process. So how can we develop understanding of our creativity?

To cope with this dilemma, we search for the shared experiences among creative women. One common feeling is uncertainty, especially during the early stages of developing the creative self. One client described it best when she lamented, "I realize I'm on the right path, but sometimes I don't know whether I'm stepping into quicksand or onto a rock." Feeling insecure is normal as we experiment with our creativity, but these doubts can interfere with fully developing our process. And they can arise both externally and internally.

People and events may contribute to our insecurity as we expose our efforts to the scrutiny of others. By its nature, creativity challenges the status quo, questions the correctness of procedures, and generally upsets the usual order of things. The resulting change can disturb and even frighten people. The instigator of change, the creative individual, is frequently viewed with a combination of respect, envy, suspicion, and resentment. Yet our progress as a civilization comes from the minds of creative people.

It's no wonder the creator can feel unsure of herself internally. Risk-taking, along with its accompanying misgivings, forms an inherent part of the creative process. The personal feelings tied to women's work mean that putting forth our creative efforts is committing an act of self-exposure. There are no guarantees of success and acceptance.

Uncertainty can become fear—fear of the unknown as we experience a new part of ourselves, fear of self-exposure as we make public our inner feelings, or fear of success. By staying attuned to our creative selves when these feelings arise, we can move forward in spite of them.

When we were first inspired to pursue creative endeavors or to develop a creative lifestyle, no uncertainty existed. We had complete trust in ourselves and our efforts. It was a solid rock to stand on. But when we encounter blocks or allow others to discourage us, we can begin feeling shaky. We may question our ability to be creative, breaking down trust in the creative process and transforming our path of rock into quicksand.

The key to overcoming self-doubt is confidence in our process. Women tell me repeatedly that trusting themselves is critical to their creative success. They learn to count on their process to come up with ideas when needed, to subconsciously work out problems with a project, and to protect themselves from going public before they are emotionally detached from the product. As Lillian, a counselor, put it, "I rely on my own deep sense of self-trust! Being creative always leaves my 'gut' feelings soothed and satisfied."

This level of trust doesn't happen quickly. And unfortunately our fast-paced society teaches us that difficulties ought to be resolved in thirty minutes—with time out for commercials! Developing confidence in our creative abilities takes time.

Regardless of the specific issue being faced, the best place to start is with the original inspiration that triggered your creative enthusiasm. Remember the moment when your entire being, head and body, said, "Yes, that's what I want to do." This spirit recaptures the trust that sparked the process. The following activity helps you get back to that feeling.

> Close your eyes and center yourself with several minutes of deep breathing. Let extraneous thoughts or concerns leave your mind.
>
> Now allow your breathing to take you to that moment when you first felt inspired to pursue the line of work or the particular project you're now beginning to question. Recall it as vividly as possible, seeing, hearing, smelling, tasting, and feeling the inspiration.
>
> Let this sensation move throughout your body, from your toes and the tips of your fingers to the top of your head. Stay with the feeling until you're certain that when you open your eyes, you'll still feel it. Give yourself plenty of time for the enthusiasm to fill your body.
>
> Slowly open your eyes, becoming aware of your surroundings while holding on to your confident feelings. If you sense the good feelings fading, close your eyes and call them back. Do this until you can resume your creative work with your confidence intact.

If fear is an issue for you, think of a roller coaster or a darkened fun house. Why do so many people enjoy these attractions even though a lot of screaming happens? The fear of apparitions in the dark or racing downhill, twisting violently in one direction and then another, becomes excitement. These two emotions—fear and excitement—are essentially the same, except excitement is fun! They are simply experienced from a different perspective. Of course, I'm not talking about the fear of walking alone down a dark alley. That concern has to do with physical well-being. I'm talking about the fear that accompanies change. It's an emotional state that can be respected without being crippling.

So the challenge when confronting fear is turning it into excitement. Try this sentence-completion technique to help you clarify your concerns. Write out the sentence as many times as you need.

> "My fear is . . . ." or "I'm afraid of . . . ."
> Next, using the sentence you've written, change the word *fear* to *excitement.*
> "My excitement is about . . . ." or "I'm excited about . . . ."
> Continue writing about any feelings and/or thoughts stirred up as you go through this activity.

People frequently resist the notion that they can be enthusiastic about something they were afraid of. But give yourself time to consider this possibility. Once you've elevated fears to excitement, you'll be able to move ahead with new energy, enthusiasm, and renewed trust. The trick is to look at the fear and ask yourself, "Where, within this fear, is the excitement?"

Opening communication between you and your creativity will help solidify your confidence in the process. One way to accomplish this involves talking with your creative self. In this case, I suggest you dialogue in writing. Dialoguing is a way of opening up a part of ourselves that we want to get to know better. It's a common technique in dream work. ◀ Admittedly, it's a bit strange, but dialoguing is a very effective skill to have. This next activity may seem unusual at first. After all, talking to ourselves has been discouraged by many well-meaning mental-

See
Letting Your Dreams Create for You
p. 187

health professionals. Still, this type of inner dialogue is powerful. You will be having a conversation between you and your creative self, asking it all kinds of getting-to-know-you questions. The easiest way is writing out the dialogue, designating each speaker. Use the medium that is comfortable for you: pen and paper, typewriter, or computer.

> Begin by writing out a question you want to ask your creative self. Avoid posing "why" questions since the usual responses are rambling rationalizations. Your dialogue might look like this:
>
> Me: Creative Self, I'm having trouble trusting you. What can I do?
>
> C.S.: Relax. And stop expecting so much of yourself. And remember, we have a very positive history together.
>
> Me: That's true. We do. I need your advice on how to relax and nurture you at the same time.
>
> C.S.: Taking play breaks would be good.
>
> Continue with the dialogue until you feel finished. When you conclude, be sure to thank your creative self for talking with you.

You may feel awkward at first, as if you're forcing the answers, but stick with it. You'll eventually reach the point of knowing what your creative self has to say only as you are writing. When this happens, the writing will feel smooth and unforced. The more often you engage your creative self in conversation, the better rapport you'll develop with this uniquely powerful aspect of yourself.

We also build trust in our process as we use it. While I can give you guidelines about how to develop your relationship with your creativity, get through blocks, and overcome the pitfalls inherent in the process we share, the particulars of the relationship are unique to you. You'll become intimately familiar with those specifics as you express your creativity. Conversely, the more you trust it, the more reliable it will be. Creativity flourishes when it's noticed and expressed.

Honesty to ourselves is another element creative women possess that reinforces trust. We have to express what is within us in ways that are right for us. As one woman told me, "I trust myself to understand what comes and to be truthful." Commercial considerations come later, if at all. When we maintain integrity about our work, we trust our efforts and our process as extensions of our true selves. This path is solid, indeed.

Part Four
Breaking Blocks

Overcoming Blocks

We've all heard about writer's block—a dreaded, mysterious malady striking innocent authors without warning and disrupting the writing process for as long as it pleases. It willfully comes and goes and has no known antidote. This phenomenon isn't confined to writers; anyone's creativity can be similarly disrupted. The common view of blocks sees them as a natural and therefore unavoidable part of the creative process. Many people maintain some paralyzing notions about blocks, as if the phenomenon held some power over both the creative process and the creator. These views ignore a critical element: the creative process is intended to flow smoothly. Struggle is an add-on! Blocks are not inherent in the process and can be stopped or even avoided in the first place.

Certainly, feeling stymied in our creative process has happened to all of us. It can be frustrating, knowing that within ourselves wonderful, exciting ideas are just waiting to burst forth. We can feel them inside, lightly tickling our consciousness with a sensation somewhere between irritation and pleasure. They're just below the surface. Just beyond the grasp of our awareness. Sound familiar?

Anything inhibiting or stopping the natural flow of creativity can be called a block. Obstacles occur for different reasons and at varying levels in the creative process. Regardless of the particulars, what we're trying to accomplish as we deal with blocks is re-establishing our flow of creative energy.

The more we experience our creativity and the more we trust our process, the less of a problem we'll have with blocks. Portia Nelson, who expresses her creativity in many ways, describes how she deals with blocks: "I meditate as much as possible and try to let go of any obsessive feelings—I trust that what's right will show up. It usually does."

As we get to know our creative selves, we'll learn how we allow ourselves to become blocked. With this understanding, we can figure out how to overcome the block. Generally, we encounter more blocks while we're developing our creativity than we do after several years of working with it.

During the many workshops I've conducted on breaking through blocks, I've found a distinct difference between people who have made extensive use of their creativity and those with less experience. The former agree most of their blocks happen when they're procrastinating. They simply need to exercise self-discipline to get the process going. The less-experienced creators, however, encounter a variety of blocks and have to learn more coping techniques.

The clearer our relationship with our creativity, the less likelihood of encountering severe stoppages in the process. As we allow the energy of the creative process—our passion—to take over, we tap into our naturally occurring motivation for doing creative work. This force melts away blocks. The following example shows what can happen when we allow our creativity its full expression.

Several years ago an artist-friend speculated that she intentionally blocked herself from starting on a painting because of the impact it had on her life. "Once I start on a painting, everything else in my life stops. I don't answer the phone; I don't socialize. I'm painting twelve to fourteen hours a day. I hate not seeing my friends, but when you've got to paint, you've got to paint! Finally, I realized that I have some blocks that stop me from working so my life won't undergo such radical changes." So sometimes a block may seem to be doing us a favor by keeping us from disrupting our lives.

In recent discussions, this same artist says it's been "eons" since she felt blocked. Her problem now is having so many ideas that choosing which one to work with is difficult. She also accepts her needs while painting, feeling comfortable with the introverted nature of her life.

While researching creativity, I found many references drawing a parallel between the creative process and the cycle of life, death, and rebirth.[1, 2, 3] This concept says that when experiencing the deepest levels of creativity, some part of the creator dies. At the end of the entire process, however, the individual is reborn a more whole, mature person. Understandably, this grand view of creativity is usually tinged with fear. If we accept this attitude as we work with our creativity, we may effectively block ourselves from the deep levels of our process. But by staying in our feminine perspective, we understand life, death, and rebirth as a part of the same cycle. ◄ And we recognize that ingression—going within ourselves—is a natural aspect of women's creative process, one that we can trust. There is nothing inherent in our process to fear.

We have to know ourselves and our process well enough to realize how to deal appropriately with interruptions in our creative process. The more we trust our process, the clearer our relationship with our creativity, and the more we allow our passions to motivate us creatively, the fewer problems we'll have with blocks.

The next five chapters, devoted to distinctive types of blocks and how to break them, are intended to put us on the road to ending blocks in our creative process.

See
Understanding Your Feminine Nature
p. 39

Trust

$\mathcal{G}$etting Started

We hold all sorts of magical things inside ourselves—ideas, poetry, stories, paintings, unique ways to solve problems. Our challenge lies in finding the path to allow the magic out, to express our creative selves. But the blank page, the empty computer screen, the naked canvas, or even the anticipation of beginning with nothing and ending with some product can set our thoughts and feelings into a swirl through which creativity can't pass. Getting started can be intimidating. Have you ever felt like that? How did you cope?

Blocks to Getting Started

When we begin a new project, we may stymie ourselves in differing ways. For example, if we look at the entire project at once, we might become overwhelmed by the many steps necessary to complete it. We're obsessed with the holistic perspective and we lose our ability to organize linearly. Or we can focus exclusively on the details of the project, forfeiting the broader picture of how those details fit into a harmonious whole. In this instance, the linear dominates at the expense of the holistic and nothing seems connected. Our holistic and linear processes are at odds, one completely overshadowing the other. We need to blend the two so they complement each other and help us express our creativity.

Sometimes we expect whatever comes out of our mouths, pens, or brushes to be exactly the way we want it to be, no corrections needed.

Challenges

We think and rethink, formulate and reformulate until we believe our creation will be perfect. In the meantime, our creative flow has been stopped.

Our products will always need polishing. Expecting them to emerge in ideal form puts a stifling burden on our creativity. Initially, the important thing is getting the ideas on paper or sketching the painting. Only after we've expressed ourselves will we have something to refine. As Marjory, a writer, described her experience, "Once I start writing, I'm usually OK. Often I will just start typing nonsense—a stream of words that have no meaning—and that seems to prime the pump."

Your dilemma may be solved simply by reminding yourself that polishing comes later. Creativity rarely expresses itself perfectly the first time around. Take comfort in this thought!

Stimulating Your Creative Juices

If you find yourself struggling to get started, try some of the following activities, all of which are designed to "prime your pump" and get you going. The first activity asks you to express in writing what you are experiencing. Following this example may be helpful:

> You might write something like, "I'm having a hard time starting this letter. I just don't know what to write. What I'd like to say is . . . ." You may have to go on for several sentences or pages, noting your frustrations, doubts, or other feelings. As you externalize them, you clear these blocks out of the path of your creativity.
>
> If you're feeling overwhelmed by either your holistic or linear process at the expense of the other, the same technique can be used. You might start with, "I'm feeling bewildered by this project. There are so many things to

do. I don't know where to start. One place I could begin is . . . ." Choose the wording to suit your needs.

Sometimes unusual techniques may be necessary to stimulate your creative juices: writing anything that comes to mind, drawing, writing or drawing with your nondominant hand, or even altering your sense of time. The following drawing technique is especially useful in helping shift perspectives and break out of blocks arising from a limited vision. ◄

See
**Making the
Ordinary
Extraordinary**
p. 169

For this activity, start with several large pieces of newsprint and some crayons, pastels, colored pencils, or even finger paints. Focus on the problem or project by closing your eyes and breathing deeply. Don't worry about the venture or be preoccupied about being unable to get started. Now ask for a symbolic image of your task. Be patient, allowing ample time for your imagery to be activated. As soon as you have the symbol(s) or when you feel like it, begin to draw. You don't need to understand the image yet. And remember, this is a symbolic drawing, so it doesn't have to look like a particular object. Simply try to capture the essence of the image.

If you have allowed sufficient time for a symbol to be presented and you sense nothing, begin drawing anyway. *Don't think.* Just let your hand choose the colors and make the drawing.

Using the same techniques, make another drawing of how the problem would look if it were solved or how the project might appear if it were finished. *It doesn't matter if you don't know exactly what the solution or final product is!*

Or you might want to draw the process of reaching a solution. This drawing can fill the gap between the problem and the final solution. Again, it's best to draw symbols to represent the process.

Working with someone else on this activity can be helpful. Each of you can create your own representations and then discuss them. Talk about what the drawings mean to you as well as any feelings that came up about the project while you were drawing. If you're working alone, write down your impressions of the drawing and what it tells you about the project.

At this point, the pump should be primed and your creative juices should be flowing. You're ready to begin actual work on the issue.

Have fun with this activity and avoid tripping yourself up with the expectation that these drawings should be of museum quality. If you find yourself having trouble starting the drawings, use your nondominant hand. Negative messages about drawing are tracked into the dominant hand and arm, the one you were using when you received the messages. The other arm and hand don't have these negative tapes or the high expectations.

And think as little as possible. These activities work best when the drawings seem to come from "nowhere." Try letting your spontaneous self have its way and avoid analyzing or rationalizing. These same suggestions hold for professional artists having similar difficulty.

Try this next activity, which is similar to the writing experience a few pages back except that you're drawing instead.

Begin by doodling or sketching anything. Avoid expectations of these practice pieces turning into great works of art. Be outrageous! Draw things sideways or upside down or at odd angles. Try unusual colors, like purple trees with orange leaves against a green sky. The idea is to stimulate your creative process, connecting it with the project at hand.

Another technique for getting started requires the use of the feminine's fluid sense of time. ◄ The feminine experiences time just as Nature does: events are connected, one flowing into another. This experience of time is different from our adopted clock sense in which events seem to happen in isolation. Our feminine sense of time enables us to move into the future, to the point where our project is complete. We can create the present from the future. In the following activity, we're beginning at the end. The book is written, the report submitted, the painting finished.

See
Altering Your Sense of Time
p. 119

Begin by closing your eyes and focusing on your breathing. Follow your breath in with your attention and follow it back out. Do this for several minutes until you feel centered and relaxed, then let your breathing return to normal.

Now imagine yourself moving forward in time to when you have finished your current project. (Sometimes people actually have the sensation of moving.) When you feel as if you've arrived at the completion point, begin noticing tangible things. What time is it? What's the date? You may have moved a few hours or several days or weeks ahead. Where are you? You might be in your office or studio or in a meeting with others. Or you may be at home where you've just received a copy of your published book. Give yourself time to note your surroundings, to truly be in that moment. Notice many details about your physical surroundings.

Next, focus your attention on your finished project, experiencing it as vividly as possible. Hold the book. Read a few pages. Touch the painting. You might even be able to smell the fresh paint. See the solution being carried out. If others are involved, note who is accomplishing which tasks and how each one fits together to form the solution. Give yourself enough time to make the finished product real to you.

With a clear image and strong sense of the final product, open your eyes and begin to create.

While this activity may seem unusual, it accomplishes three major goals. First, it shifts you out of a place of stagnation by altering your usual sense of clock time. Second, it enables you to reaffirm within yourself that you can and will complete the task. Third, it activates your imagination in service to your creativity.

Throughout these activities, reassure yourself that you hold inside all the magic, all the creativity, and all the energy you need to successfully complete the project, solve the problem, write the memo or novel, or paint the picture.

Procrastination and Creativity— Working Together

Wasting Time and Creativity

"I'll just do this one more thing, then I'll start working." How many times has this thought run through our heads? We intend to begin a project, but instead we take time to make a phone call or water a plant or stop at a co-worker's desk. Then we find one more thing to do, effectively preventing ourselves from starting the project by attending to little chores and avoiding the priority. I reached my ultimate in procrastination the morning I found myself washing out my washing machine instead of writing!

Procrastination, a common block afflicting most of us, has several causes. If the task we're about to begin requires intensive work, we may hesitate because of the commitment of time and energy. Once we're into it, other activities, including enjoyable ones, will have to be delayed.

We may fail to understand priorities, genuinely believing we ought to do the little chores before starting on the big project. But most lives contain endless small diversions. When we find ourselves distracted by getting one more drink of water, making a not-so-important phone call, or composing a memo that could have been written later, we need to recognize we're simply procrastinating. If the project is the most important task, that's where our efforts belong.

One small diversion can become a significant hindrance to starting creative work. Even after we've established our sacred space and time, we're responsible for getting ourselves into that space at a particular time. ◄ Working at home can have as many distractions as working in a traditional office. Sometimes it's easier to procrastinate when no one else is around to see what we're doing or not doing. My general rule is if something in my home is on fire, putting out the flames takes priority. Otherwise, writing comes first.

See
A Room of Your Own
p. 83

Developing Self-Discipline

Self-discipline is the key to coping with procrastination. While spontaneity is important in stimulating creativity, creating is hard work, requiring more self-discipline than any other endeavor. This runs contrary to a popular concept of creative work happening under conditions of unrestricted spontaneity. Thomas Edison's notion of genius as 1 percent inspiration and 99 percent perspiration applies here. Ginia, who runs an import business and paints and writes, knows about this issue: "I'm a firm believer in not waiting for the muse, but that no matter what mood I'm in, once I start a creative process things will start to click and other concerns will fall away."

Sometimes we need a strict schedule to control our time and motivate us to work. I often use the following technique when I'm beginning a project requiring me to use my time differently from how I've been using it. Every minute of the day is planned.

Begin with the time you get up in the morning. Note the length of time spent eating breakfast, exercising, showering, driving to work. Be sure to include all the activities you have to complete before you can begin working. Write out the schedule for the entire day, including meal breaks, drive times, and relaxation periods, through bedtime. During the periods you've blocked out for creative work, do nothing but that work, being as spontaneously creative as you want. Your schedule will probably vary from day to day, but it should always contain significant time for creative work. The morning might look something like this:

6 a.m.	Get up!
6–6:30	Coffee and newspaper
6:30–7	Exercise
7–7:30	Breakfast
7:30–8	Shower
8-noon	Write
Noon–12:30	Lunch

A schedule is especially important for anyone working at home, where too many tempting distractions can be found. If you have an outside job and are trying to do creative work during your off-hours, having a plan of activities is critical. After using your schedule for a while, you may have to make adjustments. Have you allowed too much time for particular activities, or not enough? Are work and play balanced?

I admit that, like so many creative people, I don't like scheduling my time so tightly. But I also know I need help with discipline and structure around time. This technique gives me the framework I need.

After formulating this daily plan, the next challenge is sticking with it. If you've planned to be at your desk working from nine to noon, as much as your situation allows, you must ignore phone calls or other interruptions during that time. You may also have to refuse friends' invitations to go out. This is, after all, your sacred time.

I've found that many people discover they have more time than they realized as they construct this schedule. "Wasted time" disappears. I've also observed that initially most people have to look at their schedules each day to help them stick to their plan, but after a while, the schedule becomes automatic. The joy of doing creative work takes over, there's less of a struggle with discipline, and the schedule becomes a way of living.

Prioritizing

Within this framework, chunks of time are devoted to creative activities. This works well for concentrating on one project, but what happens when we have to juggle several tasks at once? Too often, we start on one chore, then begin thinking about the other things we have to do. So we'll stop working and jump to another task. From there we usually leap to another and so on until our energy is scattered and nothing is completed. Stress goes up, efficiency goes down, and creativity is nowhere around. Have you been in that situation?

Sometimes, saying "no" to multiple tasks can be the answer to spreading our creative energies too thinly. But we may also need to learn skills for managing our commitments. The following activity combines prioritizing with exercising self-discipline.

The first step is to make a complete list of tasks you need to work on today. Next, each responsibility on your list must be prioritized. Most people try to look at the whole list at the same time, comparing everything at once. This is the toughest way to prioritize. The most effective method I've found was developed by John Crystal and Richard Bolles in *Where Do I Go from Here with My Life?* and is designed to compare each item with every other item on the list.[1]

Starting with your list, number each task. You're going to compare two items at a time, deciding between those two which one is more important. So, comparing numbers 1 and 2, put a check mark beside the more important one. Next, compare numbers 1 and 3, checking your choice there. Work your way through your list, comparing number 1 to each task and making your choice. Now go back to number 2 and compare it to number 3, checking the more important. Go through the list again, this time comparing number 2 with each item. Continue this process until you've looked at each task in comparison to every other task.

Your list might look something like this:

1. Finish report   √ √ √
2. Meet with Sally   √
3. Start working on proposal
4. Call Jack   √ √
5. E-mail committee about next meeting   √ √ √ √

Now count the number of check marks for each item. The one with the most checks will be your top priority for the day. And you'll have the remaining tasks ordered as well. If you happen to have a tie, the one you selected when you compared them will take precedence. Rewrite your list, this time with the items ranked in importance.

1. E-mail committee about next meeting
2. Finish report
3. Call Jack
4. Meet with Sally
5. Start working on proposal

From this approach, you can plainly see that the first thing you want to do is E-mail the committee. Then you want to finish the report. Only when you've completed that task are you ready to call Jack and then meet with Sally. Starting on the proposal doesn't need to concern you until after you've finished the other tasks. You may not even get to it today. And that's OK.

While this activity will quickly result in a prioritized task list, you'll still need to exercise self-discipline in your follow-through. *Once you begin working on the most important item, you must stay with it until you're finished!* This is the key. Even if you spend the entire day on one task, you're working on the most important thing. The others can wait. Put them out of your mind. If you're tempted to start hopping from project to project, remember: scattered energy blocks you from being effective and efficient.

I first discovered the importance of this approach years ago while working on my master's degree. Over half my work was independent study, so I had to learn to pace my work on my own. I faithfully made out my list every evening for the following day. By the end of the next day, I was always surprised to find some of the unattended items on the current list didn't appear on the next one. Somehow, they had taken care of themselves or they simply weren't important enough. This style of working can help us attune to what is important in our lives and teach us to use our energy appropriately.

Backsliding

In spite of our best intentions to limit procrastinating, we'll occasionally backslide. Sometimes events seem to conspire to pull us off our schedule. Or we just can't focus our attention on the task. Whatever the reason, it happens.

When you experience yourself backsliding, be kind. You can beat yourself up over it, "See, I knew you couldn't do it." That nagging little voice that loves to point out faults can have a great time. You can use the situation as an excuse to quit or as an opportunity to face self-doubts by reaffirming your intention to pursue your creative work. You can assert, "I'm strong and committed to my creative intentions." The next day, resume your schedule.

Remember, you're learning new behaviors, working to take power away from things that have blocked you in the past, and reclaiming your connections to your creative self. This takes time and patience along with the discipline to stay with techniques that will help you achieve these goals.

Creative Procrastination

We procrastinate by submitting to diversions out of habit, lack of discipline, or failing to honor our priorities. But another kind of stalling can happen, coming less from our conscious awareness and more from our subconscious. I call this phenomenon *creative procrastination*. It occurs when we have done everything right—and still can't get started: we're sitting at the computer or our desk, we've disciplined ourselves to honor our sacred space and time, and we've given ourselves ample time to begin the project. We've even tried various techniques to get the creativity flowing, but nothing is working. This resistance usually happens when we've been pushing ourselves too hard. We may fail to recognize we're exhausted, but some part of us does have this awareness and simply shuts down the process. We need to take a break from work and engage in some completely different activity—a movie, dancing, exercising, a change of scenery.

Unlike other types of stalling, creative procrastination has a healthy intent at its source. Some part of our psyche is trying to prevent us from

Nurturing
Yourself

burning out. But knowing when we're putting off work for an unhealthy reason and when we're doing it for our own good requires understanding ourselves as creative individuals. Experience tells us when we're doing which.

Creative procrastination enables the imaginative part of the brain to work on a problem while we're relaxing, encouraging the synthesis of various parts of the task. So when we return to the project after taking a break, our creativity ought to flow smoothly. We may even be surprised at how much work we can accomplish with amazingly little effort. Avoiding the work from lack of discipline won't produce the same results. What was a grind before taking a break will still be drudgery.

We also have to give ourselves a reasonable amount of time with the project before deciding creative procrastination is called for. If I sit at my computer for forty-five minutes to a hour and nothing has happened and I realize I've been working steadily for several days without a relaxing break, then I know it's time to do something else for a few hours. On the other hand, if I begin thinking about taking a hike or running errands before I've even made an effort to work, I know I'm simply procrastinating for no sound purpose.

Knowing whether we're procrastinating for healthy or unhealthy reasons determines how we'll deal with this block. As we learn to distinguish between the two, we'll become clearer in our relationship with our creative self.

Quieting the Inner Critic

"You can't start this section with a quote; you did that in the last one." My inner critic nags at me. I freeze . . . then erase what I've written. That voice, always ready to tell me when I'm doing something "wrong," has stopped my creative process. And I'm not alone in this phenomenon.

Almost everyone has an inner critic, developed from hearing well-intentioned parents, teachers, and coaches point out our errors. We internalize the negative messages, voiced every time we make a "mistake." Creative expression rarely happens without mistakes. Apparently Mozart needed little polishing of his works, but the rest of us must edit, refine, rework, revise, and improve what we've created until we're satisfied. But this work can't happen in the midst of the creative process. The inner critic, heard during the act of creation, inhibits the process. Ideas and expressions of feelings can't flow freely where they are scrutinized upon inception.

A comment made by a client typifies the influence of the inner critic. This woman worked in business for over fourteen years, rising to upper management. She was exploring ways to enliven her by-now-routine job. Although she had published several articles in her area of expertise, she resisted encouragement from me to pursue more writing. She threw out a few weak objections before she finally said, "It's too hard to write.

I keep having to stop and fix everything as I go." This approach robbed her of the joy of the creative process. I began teaching her how to deal with her critical part.

Put It on the Shelf

The inner critic serves an important function while fine-tuning our creative endeavors or when evaluating the positives and negatives of ideas generated in a brainstorming session. Honoring it for the valuable role it can play is important; in the meantime, however, it needs to be quieted. Instead of caving in to its negative criticisms or wasting energy fighting them, we can make friends with this part of ourselves. Not everything it has to say is helpful, but it often contains valuable information about rules of grammar, color and balance, or what will work in one idea and what won't in another. So acknowledging when and how it can be useful goes a long way to stilling this fault-finding voice.

Because this is a part of ourselves, we want to approach it with respect. The inner critic has its usefulness as well as its drawbacks. Keeping this perspective is important as we encounter it. The next activity is designed to help you communicate your needs to your inner critic.

≈

Begin to take control of your inner critic by getting an image of it. What does it look like? You may need to close your eyes to see this image. Give yourself time for the picture to develop. You may see a human figure or some unidentifiable form.

What does the voice sound like? You've probably heard it often enough. Conjure up as vivid a picture of your inner critic as you can. Now start a dialogue with it. You may want to conduct this discussion in writing, out loud (you probably ought to be alone if you choose this option), or inside your head. Acknowledge the positive things your inner critic can help you accomplish: editing, evaluating ideas, generally improving your creative works.

Now explain how it interferes with your creative process by interrupting the flow at inappropriate times. These actions are what you want to be rid of, not the entire inner critic. It needs to understand this. If it thinks you're trying to destroy it completely, it'll fight hard for its life and you'll have an extremely difficult task in trying to quiet it. So clearly explain that you want to keep the beneficial aspects and mute the destructive ones, that there's a time for it to speak and a time to be silent.

To accomplish this separation while you're working, ask your inner critic to be quiet if it starts nagging. Initially, you'll probably have to use more force than simply asking for silence. You may have to imagine putting it on a shelf, outside your office, or even outdoors. (I used to have to put mine into a brown burlap bag, tie it with a drawstring, then put it outside.) Always remind your inner critic you'll invite it back when you need it.

The first few times you do this, your critical part may kick up a fuss. But as it learns to trust that it'll be called upon when it can be useful, temporarily silencing it will be easier. Without the distractions of the inner critic, your creative process will flow more smoothly. By using the constructive aspects of this judgmental part, your efforts in polishing your work will be more effective.

Countering Criticism with Affirmations

Dealing with the inner critical voice will lead to another important improvement in your creative work: by coping with it internally, you won't unconsciously project your inner critic out to be reflected back by others. For example, if you deny your critical part, telling yourself it doesn't exist or isn't important, you may hear people around you voicing its criticisms. You can find yourself surrounded by people telling you how hard it is to be successful pursuing your creative work or reminding you of past projects that didn't work out as planned. Anything your inner critic would say will be verbalized by others. To avoid externalizing the inner critic, acknowledge it and establish a relationship with it.

Rejections can stimulate the inner critic, giving it fuel to run its criticisms. Be ready for this possibility by having positive statements in mind to counter the negativity. When the critical voice tries to play on your feelings of being rejected, you can be ready with an affirmation about your creative intent. A negative statement from your inner critic like, "See, I knew this idea was dumb. Nobody's going to want to use it," can be countered with, "I create solid, valuable ideas that work for my company."

You've been with your inner critic long enough to know what kinds of things it will say under these circumstances. So you can figure out ahead of time the affirmations you want to use. Your intent with these statements is to counter the part of yourself that believes the negative assertion. To be effective, they must contain positive, simple language. Avoid using ambiguous words such as "good" which can have too many meanings. Your affirmations should be stated in present tense, as if the conditions you're affirming already exist.

Putting these suggestions in writing will help you to gain control over the critical statements. Try the following activity:

Divide a sheet of paper into two columns. In the right column, list all the statements your inner critic makes that are destructive to you. It may say things like, "You're not good enough." "See, I told you you couldn't succeed." "Watch out. You better not do that. You'll get hurt." Continue adding to the list until you think you've got all the statements.

Now in the left column, write out a positive affirmation to counter the negative. You might write, "I am a competent person." "I enjoy succeeding in many ways." "I move forward with confidence."

As you are writing the positives, say them over to yourself, connecting them with equally healthy feelings. To be effective, the affirmation must be connected to the desired feeling.

The next time your inner critic attacks you, you can counter with your positive affirmation, saying the words and feeling the feelings.

Or you might want to take one affirmation and work with it, using the following guidelines:

When you use your affirmation is crucial to its effectiveness. Any time you have some shock to your system, you're in an excellent situation to accept your affirmation. The stimulus can be minor: a paper cut, an altercation in traffic where you've had to react quickly, stubbing your toe, the shift in consciousness that happens as you're falling asleep or waking up. These are all excellent times to repeat your affirmation because your logical processes are temporarily muted. They can't rally your inner critic to discount your positive statement about yourself. When this state occurs, simply repeat your affirmation over and over, allowing the healthy feeling to move through you. You're literally laying down a new track in your brain, geared to believing the positive about you. Eventually, one affirmation takes its place in your belief system and you can begin working with a different one.

Be careful with affirmations. They're powerful. You'll get what you affirm, especially using them as I've suggested here. And concentrate on only one at a time. Your psyche is involved in this process, and once again you're asking it to change. You'll overwhelm it if you use more than one statement at a time.

It usually takes several weeks with one affirmation for you to genuinely believe it. Several changes can let you know when that belief has taken hold. First, your behavior may alter in areas having to do with the affirmation. For example, if you're affirming your ideas are valuable to your company, you may find yourself being more assertive in getting others to hear your suggestions. Or you may figure out ways to present your ideas to have a stronger impact during meetings.

Also, your inner critic won't carry the influence it used to. When it begins its tirade about your supposed inadequacies, you'll easily turn it off. Or, after some time, you'll realize it has nothing to say in situations where it previously had center stage.

I've even observed physical changes in people as their posture reflected the psychological changes. They walk in a balanced, strong manner, head erect and shoulders squared.

The critical voice can wreak havoc with our creative process, damaging self-esteem and confidence in ourselves and our creative efforts. Dealing with this nagging aspect is important to maintaining a positive sense of self as well as a healthy flow of creativity.

Dealing with
Society's Shoulds

As if the voice of the inner critic weren't enough to deal with, we have another inner message board, loaded with what we "should" be doing. Too often, these shoulds run contrary to our wants, especially when we're developing our creative process. Women's messages frequently revolve around being a good wife and mother along with being a super employee. So we hear, "You should spend more time fixing meals," and, "You should be able to handle this project by yourself." We're supposed to care for everybody else while taking charge of everything within our realm. Never mind the cost in lost creativity.

These expectations arise from childhood years of dealing with others' prescriptions for our behavior. Frequently, shoulds challenge our sense of self-worth: "Who do you think you are to question the way things have always been done? You should keep your ideas to yourself." Or the purpose for living: "What makes you think you can become a successful artist? You should be responsible and hold down a secure job!" No matter what the specific words, the effect is the same—blocked creativity and lowered self-esteem.

Our should messages generally keep us distanced from who we are as individuals and from our unique abilities. We can't explore our true selves if we're occupied with living up to everyone else's expectations. And when we do muster the courage to try something distinctive, we can cloud the experience with guilt by listening to a message about how we should be doing something different, usually directing our energy to someone else's needs.

Identifying Personal Shoulds

Sometimes our shoulds are so entwined in our behavior, we don't realize what all of them are. So our first task is identifying as many of these insidious messages as we can. Sometimes friends can help with this since their experience of us can be more objective than our own. They may "hear" shoulds in our behavior that we're blind to. Identifying and externalizing our shoulds can begin to de-power them. The following activity will help you start that process.

A useful first step in isolating shoulds is writing them down. Begin by completing the sentence "I should . . ." as many times as you can. Shoulds are attached to various activities, so think of yourself in many situations as you compile this list. Write down the shoulds connected with home, work, relationships, parents, yourself, you and your creativity.

Since a should is based upon a message taken on from the outside, it can feel as if something else has power over you when you give in to it. Taking power back from the adopted message is critical in reclaiming what you want and who you are. This is effectively accomplished by changing the language you use. Try the following activity to help you get a different perspective on your shoulds.

Working with the should list you just compiled, rewrite each message, changing the beginning of the sentence to "I want . . . ." You may not be pleased with every resulting statement. "I *should* visit my parents every week" becomes "I *want* to visit my parents every week." This may simply not be true. Convert each should, paying attention to how you react to the new language. You may want to make some alterations, such as changing the previous example to "I don't want to visit my parents every week." The message here is quite different from the original should. Now *you're* in control with the power of choice regarding your behavior.

With this new power, you also have the responsibility for the choices you make. If you allow yourself to be controlled by the should, you'll be setting yourself up to either feel guilty if you go against it or angry with yourself if you follow the should, contrary to your best interests. Conflicts with shoulds, guilt over taking care of oneself, and internalized anger are primary sources of depression in women. ◄ When you're depressed, your self-esteem suffers, making you more vulnerable to giving in to your should messages and less likely to make healthy choices.

Becoming aware of these internal messages and changing your language are major steps toward gaining control over them and neutralizing their influence over your behavior. After making a list of your shoulds, try to catch yourself repeating the message. For example, you may decide you want to do something unplanned, practicing spontaneity to stimulate your creativity. But you hear yourself saying, "Maybe I'd better not. I have a lot of things I need to do—cleaning, errands, dinner." While the word *should* doesn't appear in this message, it's implicitly understood. You should be "responsible," taking care of everything and everyone else except yourself. Meanwhile, your intention of doing something to contribute to your creative development is drowned in the

See
Understanding the Creative/ Depressive Cycle
p. 97

flood of distractions. So the real question is "What do I want to do?" Sometimes the honest answer to this question isn't the easiest. It will, however, be the healthiest.

Turning Shoulds into Wants

Once you've identified the should and understand what it's doing to you, you can tackle it by taking back the power you've given up and making a clearer choice about your behavior. Your inner dialogue in the previous example might go something like this:

"Now wait a minute. Do I want to run errands and clean the house? Do I want to fix dinner? Not really. I'm stressed out. I need to relax. There are a few things I need to pick up today, the rest can wait. I can go fly my kite for most of the afternoon, stop at the store on my way home, order a pizza for dinner, and clean tomorrow. This way I can take care of the things that really need to get done and enjoy playing. And I deserve the gift of play!"

What you say to yourself and how you say it are keys to diffusing the shoulds interfering with your personal growth and the expansion of your creative abilities. The next method for dealing with your shoulds is adapted from a Jean Houston and Robert Masters exercise.

You'll need your list of shoulds, about a half hour of your time, and either a loop tape or a friend. Record your should statements onto the tape or give them to a friend to read. Make certain you won't be interrupted during the activity, and you're ready to begin.

Start by focusing on your breathing, following your breath in with your awareness and following it out. Do this for several minutes, until your attention is completely on you. Now imagine yourself engaged in your creative work. Pull as many senses as you can into play, seeing yourself engaged in the activity or the endeavor, feeling your muscles doing the creative work, smelling the scents around you, hearing the sounds, tasting coffee or whatever you might drink while working. Immerse yourself in expressing your creativity. Physically move around if that helps make the experience more vivid for you. Give yourself plenty of time to build the sensation of being engaged in your creative work.

When you feel yourself saturated in your creative process, turn on the tape or indicate to your friend to start reading your shoulds. Stay with your creative work as you are bombarded over and over with these negative messages. Can you stay focused and for how long? Do some statements pull you away from your intent more than others? Is it easier or harder to be with your creative work as you hear more messages?

After ten to fifteen minutes of listening to shoulds, shut off the tape or quiet your friend. Return to a solid image of being engaged in your creative work. Then open your eyes and return to the room.

Make note of the shoulds carrying the most influence, the ones tending to pull you off track. Plan ways to deal with them as they come up for you. What will you say to yourself to diffuse the should when it makes itself heard? Repeat this activity as often as you feel necessary. You'll find the shoulds losing power after a while as you have an easier time staying committed to your creative work.

Most of our should messages were accepted without question as they were given to us by the authority figures in our lives. They block creativity by depleting our energy, not allowing room for the self-attention required to develop the creative process, while encouraging us to stay within the expected societal norm which discounts our distinctive abilities. But with vigilance we can assert our power to make positive choices as we live our creative lifestyle.

Dancing with Goliath

We all know the scene: a huge, stiff-legged monster lumbers toward his trembling victim, one slow step at a time. His rigid elbows bend awkwardly as he lifts his weapon. To look right or left, he must turn his entire torso. This unwieldy being contains about as much intelligence as he does coordination. Yet his victims, frozen with fear, fall before him. If only they'd exercised their superior agility, they could have easily outmaneuvered the galumphing villain.

Blocks to our creativity can also inspire fear and move with the slow clumsiness of a monster. When we're blocked, we can feel as if we're dancing with Goliath. So we need to change the dance.

A New Way of Dancing

Blocks in the creative process are often obstacles to imagery.[1] Our ability to stimulate our visual, auditory, kinesthetic, or other imagery becomes clogged. We can't see possible solutions to a problem or hear characters from our novel talking with each other. The problem compounds when we focus on being blocked, feeding the interference with concern about our inability to be creative. The block that began as a mouse becomes a monster with its inexorable rhythm. Fortunately, imagery has its own rhythm and can be stimulated with sound and movement. The right dance can break blocks in imagery.

The kinds of movement we make throughout the day as adults are very different from the motions we naturally made as children. Watching three-year-olds quickly reveals the contrast. They're all over the place, crossing arms and legs from one side to the other, seemingly in perpetual chaotic motion. Jean Houston tells the story of a research project designed to see how long a professional football player in top physical form would last duplicating the movements of a three-year-old.[2] In less than fifteen minutes the athlete dropped from exhaustion as the child continued playing.

While children naturally move using cross-lateral movements, most of our adult motions are bilateral. A *cross-lateral* movement cuts across an imaginary line splitting the body in half vertically, such as swinging the right arm across the body to the left side. Cross-lateral movements have the effect of stimulating the learning centers in the brain. *Bilateral* motion, on the other hand, is confined to one side of the body, the right arm moving forward on the right side, for example. While vigorous bilateral movements, like those we use bicycling or running, increase the oxygen in the brain by pumping more blood, they don't do anything to stimulate learning or creativity.

Right now, try a few minutes of a cross-lateral movement exercise designed by Robert Masters and Jean Houston. Give yourself lots of room; I don't want you to slam your foot into your desk. If you're wearing high heels, I suggest taking them off so you won't be in danger of falling over!

Start by swinging your left foot over your right, then swing your right foot over your left. Do this many times, establishing a rhythm. Next add your arms, swinging in the opposite direction from your legs. Now follow your feet with your head so both are moving in one direction while your arms are going in the opposite direction. If you lose the pattern, stop everything, then start with the feet and build.

To add additional interest, image yourself eating a favorite food, watching a colorful sunset, and petting your cat all at the same time. (Naturally, you can substitute images.) Maintain this movement and imagery combination for at least five minutes.

I've taught this exercise to all ages, from teens who say it calms them down and gets their energy focused to senior citizens who report that doing it daily keeps them energized. The technique I've described here is basic. You can add any variations you like, standing up or lying down, as long as you're doing cross-lateral movements.

You can use this activity almost anywhere. At work you might want to shut your office door. If you don't have your own office and can't enlist the cooperation of co-workers, perform the exercise in a restroom cubicle. It's great to do before going into a meeting. You'll be wide awake and full of good ideas. Or get everyone at the meeting to join you in five minutes of cross-lateral movements. They'll be more alert, with clearer access to their creativity.

People often add music to this activity, making it more fun and interesting. Using musical accompaniment, you'll want to give yourself plenty of room so you can invent new dance movements. Disco music is great for cross-lateral dancing. And music with unfamiliar rhythms is especially effective, since you're less likely to fall into old patterns of movement while listening to new sounds. I like to use South American folk music, such as that performed by the group Sukay.

The more vigorous your cross-lateral movements, the more stimulating to your creativity. But remember the football player. You're probably not accustomed to this type of activity, so you may quickly exhaust yourself. Since your heart rate can increase rapidly, use common sense when deciding how long and how vigorously you dance. I recommend beginning at a moderate pace, building to a faster rate. Do the activity for at least five minutes.

Most people are physically exhausted by the end of the exercise, but mentally alert. This sounds contradictory—we usually expect if our body is exhausted, we'll be ineffective mentally, too. Because of the way cross-lateral movements affect the brain, we can be physically tired but mentally stimulated. Our imagery centers are activated and blocks disappear. Goliath just can't keep up.

You can invent variations of this activity to help you with special challenges. For example:

> If you're grappling with a particular issue and can't seem to generate any creative ideas to deal with it, focus on that issue before beginning. Stand with your weight evenly distributed until you feel physically balanced, then close your eyes and focus on the problem. Allow it to take form so you can see it. Or sense it in your muscles. When you feel as if the issue is present, begin dancing with it, using cross-lateral movements. Actively engage in at least five minutes of vigorous activity.
>
> Now stop and notice what's happened to the problem. How did it change throughout the exercise? How do you experience the issue now? From what perspective? Do you have a solution or several possible solutions? Write them down, making notes on what happened throughout the dance.

If you're unable to physically engage in cross-lateral movements, do them in your imagination. Vividly image yourself dancing. You may feel slight sensations in your muscles. And you're stimulating your brain at the same time. Using music while you imagine the movements is just as helpful as if you were actually dancing.

Blocks don't have to take over our creativity. We can break the blocks, freeing the flow of creative energy and enabling us to utilize a unique perspective when approaching issues. Using cross-lateral movements stimulates our creative imagery, making us healthier at the same time!

A colleague described her sense of breaking through blocks. "I communicate and think many times on a frequency of color, where information just streams into my conscious in vivid color and in so many patterns that look almost like a language of their own. This generally opens a sense of passion, beauty, and love for what I am about to embark on."

Concluding Thoughts

The female hero I began searching for as a child is the self-defined, creative woman living inside each of us. When we express our true selves, we meet the world with sensitivity, not armor. Our awareness extends beyond our immediate surroundings; we're in harmony with the universe. As we live a creative lifestyle, we give voice to our feminine, trusting our inner self and asserting our unique processes as valuable to all society. Functioning on many levels of thinking at the same time becomes the norm. Linear approaches are reserved for special occasions, like balancing a checkbook.

The journey of developing our creativity is one of growth and maturation. We evolve into being self-defined, restoring balance between the masculine and the feminine, both within ourselves and in society. The authority of cultural dictates stifling to our individuality is broken. In this process we reclaim our feminine power, the power we have over ourselves. We learn that refusing to assert our inherent power is as harmful as using power to abuse others. As we become more creative in our approach to relationships, our interactions with others empower them. The path to creative living leads to wholeness and an expanded vision of our possibilities.

We experience new definitions of success as we turn fear of taking risks into excitement, learning from what we used to call mistakes. We're receptive to our own imaginations, becoming the vehicle for the creative flow of ideas, solutions, inventions, and approaches to life. We develop healthy relationships, innovative approaches to old issues, unique management styles, new literature, and works of art. But getting to this place in our lives requires effort.

We know our educational system wreaks havoc upon us early on and never lets up. It takes heroic effort to break away from our education. The holistic thinkers among our children need heroes of creativity as role models. These young people must know they're OK. One of our tasks as adults is teaching children to express themselves as creative individuals. We need to nurture a strong self-esteem in them based on their unique abilities and on the contribution those talents can make to society. The children in our homes, classrooms, families, and neighborhoods desperately need this kind of attention.

We must also attend to the child within ourselves who may not have received this kind of nurturance when she was growing up. That child is still inside, hoping to be honored for her unique abilities, wanting to be nurtured and loved unconditionally. Once we respect her needs, healing her and providing her with a voice, our inner child will be our ally every time we travel the inward journey of our creative process.

Living the creative lifestyle means a life of constant renewal. Creative expression isn't something that happens only on certain occasions in special places, like during a meeting or inside the confines of an artist's studio. The creative process is organic, interwoven throughout our every activity and thought. It requires consistent encouragement and nurturing to grow and flower. But we need to have patience with ourselves as we work to break old patterns, freeing our creative possibilities, and allowing our new self to emerge. A sense of humor and a spirit of adventure are our best companions as we cultivate our unique abilities. Once we've established a relationship with our creativity, we've developed a lasting friendship.

Learning to live creatively continues as long as we're alive. We never "arrive." When we devote ourselves to a creative lifestyle, we're committed to a life of growth directed by our creative self. We receive the greatest of all possible rewards: we become who we truly are, free of accumulated expectations. We are the female hero.

To your self-defined, creative self, I say, "Welcome."

$\mathcal{N}$otes

In the Beginning . . .

1. Graham Wallas, *The Art of Thought* (New York: Harcourt, Brace, 1926).
2. Marilyn Ferguson, *The Aquarian Conspiracy* (Los Angeles: J. P. Tarcher, 1980).
3. David Gelman, et al., "Just How the Sexes Differ," *Newsweek*, May 18, 1981, pp. 72–83.
4. Pamela Weintraub, "The Brain: His and Hers," *Discover*, April 1981, pp. 15–20.
5. Frank Barron, *Creativity and Personal Freedom* (Princeton, N. J.: D. Van Nostrand, 1968), p. 221.
6. John Gowan, *Development of the Creative Individual* (San Diego, Calif.: Robert R. Knapp, 1972), p.93.
7. Ibid., p. 55.

Getting Down to the Roots: What Is Creativity?

1. Frank Allen, "Many Bosses Already Have Decided Who Successors Will Be and Why," *The Wall Street Journal*, Nov. 18, 1980.

Finishing What You Start

1. Abraham Maslow, "The Creative Attitude," *Explorations in Creativity*, ed. Ross Mooney and Taher A. Razik (New York: Harper & Row, 1967), pp. 45–53.
2. Dr. Jean Houston, statement in workshop lecture, University of California at Santa Cruz, August 1978.

Learning to Change Reality

1. "Spurs for Innovation," *Nation's Business,* June 1986, pp. 42–45.
2. Victor Boesen, *They Said It Couldn't Be Done: The Incredible Story of Bill Lear* (Garden City, N.Y.: Doubleday, 1971).

Understanding Your Feminine Nature

1. Edith Hamilton, *Mythology: Timeless Tales of Gods and Heroes* (New York: New American Library, 1969).

2. Meyer Reinhold, *Past and Present: The Continuity of Classical Myths* (Toronto, Canada: Hakkert Ltd., 1972).

3. Charlene Spretnak, *Lost Goddesses of Early Greece* (Berkeley, Calif.: Moon Books, 1978).

4. M. Esther Harding, *The Way of All Women* (New York: G. P. Putnam's Sons, 1970).

Keep It Private—For a While

1. Judy Chicago, *Through the Flower* (Garden City, N.Y.: Doubleday, 1975), p. 142.

2. Julia M. Klein, "Quindlen to exit Times for 'dream' life as a novelist" (Knight-Ridder Newspapers), *The Arizona Daily Star*, Sept. 23, 1994, pp. 1D & 8D.

Learning to Accept Nurturance

1. Dr. Jean Houston, statement in workshop lecture, Los Angeles, Calif., March 1980.

Perfectionism: Creativity's Saboteur

1. Ellen Sue Stern, *The Indispensable Woman* (New York: Bantam, 1988), pp. 43 & 73.

2. Ibid., p. 65.

3. Ibid., p. 124.

4. Ibid., p. 134.

Understanding the Creative/Depressive Cycle

1. E. Paul Torrance, *Guiding Creative Talent* (Englewood Cliffs, N.J.: Prentice-Hall, 1962).

2. Jessie Bernard, *Women, Wives, Mothers: Values and Options* (Chicago: Aldine, 1975).

3. Ruth Formanek and Anita Gurian, eds., *Women and Depression: A Lifespan Perspective* (New York: Springer, 1987), pp. 165–67.

4. Susan Nolan-Hoeksema, *Sex Differences in Depression* (Stanford, Calif.: Stanford University Press, 1990), p. 18.

Anger: Creativity's Wrecking Ball

1. Irene C. de Castillejo, *Knowing Woman* (New York: G. P. Putnam's Sons, 1973).

2. Louise L. Hay, *You Can Heal Your Life* (Carson, Calif.: Hay House, 1994), pp. 150–88.

3. Dr. Trevor Creed, statement in workshop lecture, Tucson, Ariz., March 1990.

4. Virginia Woolf, *A Room of One's Own* (New York: Harcourt, Brace, 1929).

Altering Your Sense of Time

1. Cottle, *Perceiving Time: A Psychological Investigation with Men and Women* (New York: John Wiley & Sons, 1976).

Expanding Your Sense of Self

1. Virginia Woolf, *A Room of One's Own* (New York: Harcourt, Brace, 1929), p. 169.
2. Dr. Jean Houston, statement in workshop lecture, Los Angeles, Calif., March 1980.

Becoming a Creative Problem-Solver

1. Dr. Gay Luce, statement in workshop lecture, Los Angeles, Calif., March 1980.
2. "Spurs for Innovation," *Nation's Business,* June 1986, pp. 42–45.

Redefining Power

1. Dr. Jean Houston, statement in workshop lecture, University of California at Santa Cruz, August 1978.

Exercising Your Imagery

1. Stanislav Grof, *Realms of the Human Unconscious* (New York: Viking, 1975).
2. Jean Houston, "Through the Looking-Glass: The World of Imagery," *Dromenon* 2 (Winter 1979), pp. 17–23.
3. _____ and R.E.L. Masters, *The Varieties of Psychedelic Experience* (New York: Holt, Rinehart and Winston, 1966).

Becoming More Spontaneous

1. "Spurs for Innovation," *Nation's Business,* June 1986, pp. 42–45.
2. Brewster Ghiselin, ed., *The Creative Process* (New York: New American Library, 1952).

Making the Ordinary Extraordinary

1. Dr. Jean Houston, statement in workshop lecture, University of California at Santa Cruz, August 1978.

Loving Your Creative Self

1. Susan Campbell, *The Couple's Journey: Intimacy as a Path to Wholeness* (San Luis Obispo, Calif.: Impact, 1983).

Letting Your Dreams Create for You

1. Harriet Skibbins, statement in workshop lecture, Marin, Calif., May 1981.
2. Dr. Jean Houston, statement in workshop lecture, University of California at Santa Cruz, August 1978.
3. J. C. Cooper, *An Illustrated Encyclopedia of Traditional Symbols* (London: Thames and Hudson Ltd., 1978).

Overcoming Blocks

1. Arthur Koestler, *The Act of Creation* (New York: Macmillan, 1964).
2. _____, *Janus* (New York: Random House, 1978).
3. Rollo May, *The Courage to Create* (New York: Bantam, 1975).

Procrastination and Creativity—Working Together

1. John Crystal and Richard Bolles, *Where Do I Go from Here with My Life?* (New York: The Seabury Press, 1974).

Dancing with Goliath

1. Dr. Jean Houston, statement in workshop lecture, University of California at Santa Cruz, August 1978.
2. Ibid.

$\mathcal{B}$ibliography

Getting Down to the Roots: What Is Creativity?

Agor, Weston. *Intuitive Management: Integrating Left and Right Brain Management Skills.* Englewood Cliffs, N.J.: Prentice-Hall, 1984.

Barron, Frank. *Creativity and Personal Freedom.* Princeton, N.J.: D. Van Nostrand, 1968.

Brandt, Steven. *Entrepreneuring in Established Companies: Managing toward the Year 2000.* Homewood, Ill.: Dow Jones-Irwin, 1986.

The Holistic Process: Its Praises and Pitfalls

de Bono, Edward. *Lateral Thinking.* New York: Harper & Row, 1973.

Ealy, C Diane. *Creativity: A Feminine Perspective,* unpublished doctoral dissertation, the University for Humanistic Studies, San Diego, Calif., 1980.

Finishing What You Start

Ealy, *Creativity: A Feminine Perspective.*

Understanding Your Feminine Nature

Arguelles, Jose, and Miriam Arguelles. *The Feminine: Spacious as the Sky.* Boulder, Colo.: Shambhala, 1977.

Campbell, Joseph. *The Hero with a Thousand Faces.* Princeton, N.J.: Princeton University Press, 1949.

de Castillejo, Irene C. *Knowing Woman.* New York: G. P. Putnam's Sons, 1973.

Ealy, *Creativity: A Feminine Perspective.*

Harding, Esther. *Woman's Mysteries Ancient and Modern: A Psychological Interpretation of the Feminine Principle as Portrayed in Myth, Story and Dreams.* New York: G. P. Putnam's Sons, 1971.

Dr. Jean Houston, statement in workshop lecture, Los Angeles, Calif., March 1980.

Dr. Jean Shinoda-Bolen, statement in workshop lecture, Marin, Calif., May 1981.

Swados, Elizabeth. *The Girl with the Incredible Feeling.* U.S.A.: Persea, 1976.

Keep It Private—For a While

de Castillejo, *Knowing Woman.*

Ealy, *Creativity: A Feminine Perspective.*
Harding, M. Esther. *The Way of All Women.* New York: G. P. Putnam's Sons, 1970.
Luke, Helen. *The Life of the Spirit in Women.* Three Rivers, Mich.: Apple Farm, 1979.

Be Prepared for Provoking a Response

Ealy, *Creativity: A Feminine Perspective.*
Spretnak, Charlene. *Lost Goddesses of Early Greece.* Berkeley, Calif: Moon Books, 1978.

Learning to Accept Nurturance

Bernard, Jessie. *Women, Wives, Mothers: Values and Options.* Chicago: Aldine, 1975.
de Castillejo, *Knowing Woman.*
Harding, *The Way of All Women.*
Orsborn, Carol. *Enough Is Enough: Exploding the Myth of Having It All.* New York: G. P. Putnam's Sons, 1986.

Developing a Sense of Timing

Cottle, Thomas. *Perceiving Time: A Psychological Investigation with Men and Women.* New York: John Wiley & Sons, 1976.

A Room of Your Own

Ealy, *Creativity: A Feminine Perspective.*
Woolf, Virginia. *A Room of One's Own.* New York: Harcourt, Brace, 1929.

Perfectionism: Creativity's Saboteur

Fezler, William, and Eleanor S. Field. *The Good Girl Syndrome.* New York: Berkley, 1985.
Leman, Kevin. *Measuring Up.* Old Tappan, N.J.: Fleming H. Revell, 1988.
Simon, Sidney. *Getting Unstuck: Breaking Through Your Barriers to Change.* New York: Warner, 1988.

Understanding the Creative/Depressive Cycle

Gowan, John. *Development of the Creative Individual.* San Diego, Calif.: Robert R. Knapp, 1972.
May, Rollo. *The Courage to Create.* New York: Bantam, 1975.
Miles, Agnes. *Women and Mental Illness: The Social Context of Female Neurosis.* Brighton, Sussex, England: Wheatsheaf, 1988.
Schwartz, Lita Linzer. "Can We Stimulate Creativity in Women?" *The Journal of Creative Behavior* 11 (Fourth Quarter 1977), pp. 264–67.
Swados, *The Girl with the Incredible Feeling.*

Anger: Creativity's Wrecking Ball

Harding, *Woman's Mysteries Ancient and Modern: A Psychological Interpretation of the Feminine Principle as Portrayed in Myth, Story and Dreams.*
Luke, *The Life of the Spirit in Women.*

Altering Your Sense of Time

Dr. Jean Houston, statements in workshop lecture, Los Angeles, Calif., March 1980.

Expanding Your Sense of Self

Ealy, *Creativity: A Feminine Perspective.*
Ghiselin, Brewster, ed. *The Creative Process.* New York: New American Library, 1952.
Tart, Charles. *States of Consciousness.* New York: E. P. Dutton, 1975.

Honoring the Unmeasurable

Brandt, *Entrepreneuring in Established Companies: Managing toward the Year 2000.*
Harding, *The Way of All Women.*
Luke, *The Life of the Spirit in Women.*
Maslow, Abraham. "The Creative Attitude." *Explorations in Creativity.* Ed. Ross Mooney and Taher A. Razik. New York: Harper & Row, 1967. pp. 45–53.
_____. *The Psychology of Science.* Chicago: Henry Regnery, 1966.

Redefining Power

Ferguson, Marilyn. *The Aquarian Conspiracy.* Los Angeles: J. P. Tarcher, 1980.
Orsborn, *Enough Is Enough: Exploding the Myth of Having It All.*

Exercising Your Imagery

Assagioli, Roberto. *Psychosynthesis.* New York: Viking, 1975.
de Mille, Richard. *Put Your Mother on the Ceiling.* New York: Viking, 1975.
Ghiselin, *The Creative Process.*
Hendricks, Gay, and James Fadiman, eds. *Transpersonal Education: A Curriculum for Feeling and Being.* Englewood Cliffs, N.J.: Prentice-Hall, 1976.
Samuels, Mike, and Nancy Samuels. *Seeing with the Mind's Eye.* New York: Random House, 1975.

Ha-Ha = Aha!

Durden-Smith, Jo. "Male and Female—Why?" *Quest* (October 1980), pp. 15–98.
Ferguson, *The Aquarian Conspiracy.*
Koestler, Arthur. *The Act of Creation.* New York: Macmillan, 1964.
_____. *Janus.* New York: Random House, 1978.
Moir, Anne, and David Jessel. *Brain Sex: The Real Difference Between Men and Women.* New York: Viking Penguin, 1989.

Becoming More Spontaneous

Maslow, *The Psychology of Science.*

Parnes, Sidney J., Ruth B. Noller, and Angelo M. Biondi. *Guide to Creative Action: Revised Edition of Creative Behavior Guidebook.* New York: Charles Scribner's Sons, 1977.

Richards, Mary Caroline. *Centering in Pottery, Poetry and the Person.* 10th ed. Middletown, Conn.: Wesleyan University Press, 1978.

Making the Ordinary Extraordinary

Swados, *The Girl with the Incredible Feeling.*

Loving Your Creative Self

de Castillejo, *Knowing Woman.*

Ealy, *Creativity: A Feminine Perspective.*

Letting Your Dreams Create for You

Philip Morton, statements in workshop lecture "Dream Workshop: From the Standpoint of Jungian Psychology," Tucson, Ariz., April 1984.

Samuels, *Seeing with the Mind's Eye.*

Is It Quicksand or a Rock?

Ealy, *Creativity: A Feminine Perspective.*

Giele, Janet Zollinger. *Women and the Future.* New York: The Free Press, 1978.

Groch, Judith. *The Right to Create.* Boston: Little, Brown, 1969.

Overcoming Blocks

Erikson, Joan M. *Wisdom and the Senses: The Way of Creativity.* New York: W. W. Norton, 1988.

$\mathcal{F}$urther Readings

The following titles are suggested reading for additional information on related topics.

Anger

Campbell, Anne. *Men, Women, and Aggression.* New York: BasicBooks, 1993.

McKay, Matthew, Peter D. Rogers, and Judith McKay. *When Anger Hurts.* Oakland, Calif.: New Harbinger, 1989.

Potter-Efron, Ron. *Angry All the Time.* Oakland, Calif.: New Harbinger, 1994.

Tavris, Carol. *Anger: The Misunderstood Emotion.* New York: Touchstone, 1989.

Weisinger, Henrie. *Dr. Weisinger's Anger Work-Out Book.* New York: Quill, 1985.

Williams, Redford, and Virginia Williams. *Anger Kills.* New York: Harper Perennial, 1994.

Brain Work

Gawain, Shakti. *Creative Visualization.* New York: Bantam, 1982.

Houston, Jean. *The Possible Human.* Los Angeles: J. P. Tarcher, 1982.

Ostrander, Sheila, and Lynn Schroeder, with Nancy Ostrander. *Super-Learning 2000.* New York: Delacorte Press, 1994.

Dreams

Jung, C. G. *Dreams.* Princeton, N.J.: Princeton University Press, 1974.

The Feminine

Anderson, Sherry Ruth, and Patricia Hopkins. *The Feminine Face of God.* New York: Bantam, 1991.

Cameron, Anne. *Daughters of Copper Woman.* Vancouver, B.C., Canada: Press Gang, 1981.

Conway, D. J. *Maiden, Mother, Crone.* St. Paul, Minn.: Llewellyn, 1994.

Estes, Clarissa Pinkola. *Women Who Run with the Wolves.* New York: Ballantine, 1992.

Gadon, Elinor W. *The Once and Future Goddess.* San Francisco: HarperSanFrancisco, 1989.

Mahdi, Louise Carus, Steven Foster, and Meredith Little, eds. *Betwixt and Between: Patterns of Masculine and Feminine Initiation*. Chicago: Open Court, 1987.

Pearson, Carol S. *Awakening the Heroes Within*. San Francisco: HarperSanFrancisco, 1991.

Rutter, Virginia Beane. *Woman Changing Woman*. San Francisco: HarperSanFrancisco, 1993.

Walker, Barbara G. *Women's Rituals*. San Francisco: HarperSanFrancisco, 1990.

Ha-Ha

Kipfer, Barbara. *14,000 Things to Be Happy About*. New York: Workman, 1990.

Schaef, Anne Wilson. *Laugh—I Thought I'd Die (If I Didn't)*. New York: Ballantine, 1990.

Wagner, Jane. *The Search for Signs of Intelligent Life in the Universe*. New York: Harper & Row, 1986.

Warren, Roz, ed. *Glibquips: Funny Words by Funny Women*; *The Best Contemporary Women's Humor*; *Women's Glibber*; *Women's Glib*. Freedom, Calif: Crossing Press, 1994, 1994, 1992, 1991.

Watterson, Bill. Any of the Calvin and Hobbes books.

Meditation/Relaxation

LeShan, Lawrence. *How to Meditate*. New York: Bantam, 1974.

Levine, Stephen. *Guided Meditations, Explorations, and Healings*. New York: Doubleday, 1991.

Schaef, Anne Wilson. *Daily Meditations for Women Who Do Too Much*. San Francisco: HarperSanFrancisco, 1990.

Personal Growth

Becker, Suzy. *All I Need to Know I Learned from My Cat*. New York: Workman, 1990.

Boreggin, Peter. *Toxic Psychiatry*. New York: St. Martin's, 1994.

Borysenko, Joan. *Guilt Is the Teacher, Love Is the Lesson*. New York: Warner, 1990.

Briggs, Dorothy Corkille. *Celebrate Your Self: Enhancing Your Own Self-Esteem*. New York: Doubleday, 1977.

Gawain, Shakti. *The Path of Transformation*. Mill Valley, Calif.: Nataraj, 1993.

Gray, John. *What Your Mother Couldn't Tell You and Your Father Didn't Know*. New York: HarperCollins, 1994.

Houston, Jean. *The Search for the Beloved*. New York: Jeremy Tarcher/Perigee, 1987.

Keirsey, David, and Marilyn Bates. *Please Understand Me*. Del Mar, Calif.: Prometheus Nemesis, 1984.

Lerner, Harriet Goldhor. *Women in Therapy*. New York: Harper & Row, 1988.

Peiffer, Vera. *Positively Fearless*. Rockport, Mass.: Element, 1993.

Tannen, Deborah. *You Just Don't Understand*. New York: Ballantine, 1990.

Realizing Dreams/Careers

Chapman, Joyce. *The Live Your Dream Workbook*. North Hollywood, Calif.: Newcastle, 1994.

Jeffers, Susan. *Feel the Fear and Do It Anyway.* New York: Fawcett, 1987.

Sher, Barbara, with Barbara Smith. *I Could Do Anything if I Only Knew What It Was.* New York: Delacorte, 1994.

Wieder, Marcia. *Making Your Dreams Come True.* New York: MasterMedia Limited, 1993.

Symbolism

Jung, Carl G. *Man and His Symbols.* New York: Anchor/Doubleday, 1964.

Photo credit: Ed Flores

C Diane Ealy, Ph.D., has made a career of examining and expanding the everyday definition of the creative process. Beginning with the archaic, yet accepted, academic framework of how people were "supposed" to create, she found that the prevailing creativity models not only were confining, but they minimized the existence of the feminine process.

Ealy has been a professional speaker, author, and consultant for the past twenty years. She holds a doctorate in behavioral science and has presented more than three hundred workshops, seminars, and speeches dealing with creativity in topics ranging from "Meeting the Challenges of Change" to "Reclaiming Your Enthusiasm: Stress Management for Stressful Times" to "Women's Creativity: How to Recognize and Use Your Unique Process." She is the coauthor of *Our Money, Ourselves: Redesigning Your Relationship with Money*. Ealy also works with individual clients and corporations in expanding the role of creativity in the workplace. She can be reached at CDianeEaly@aol.com.